Guide to

Great
Wine
Values

Published by Wine Spectator Press
A division of M. Shanken Communications, Inc.
387 Park Avenue South
New York, New York 10016

Distributed by Running Press
125 South 22nd Street
Philadelphia, PA 19103

ISBN 1-881659-35-6

Wine Spectator Magazine's

Guide to
Great
Wine
Values

$10 and under

WINE SPECTATOR PRESS
A DIVISION OF M. SHANKEN COMMUNICATIONS, INC.

Foreword

T his is our
second edition of
*Wine Spectator's
Guide to Great
Wine Values*. The
first edition was so
well received last
year when it was
released, that we
quickly decided to do it again. And do it better.

The format is the same but all the great-value
wines recommended in this book are new. They need-
ed to be new because new vintages have replaced old
vintages in your wine shop, supermarket or liquor
store. To find the best buys possible, you need up-to-
date advice, and our wine reviews are the freshest
available in book form. This guide also recommends
more wines this year, over 1,150 of them.

Wine Spectator's Guide to Great WineValues
draws on the accumulated knowledge of our editorial
board to bring you informed buying advice on the
best wines you can find for $10 or less. The heart of
this book is a collection of tasting notes, with retail
prices and ratings on our 100-point scale, representing
the best recently released wines available. The ratings

and recommendations are *Wine Spectator*'s alone, stemming from independent wine tastings conducted by *Wine Spectator* magazine over the past sixteen months.

For those of you who don't know us, *Wine Spectator* is the world's largest-circulation consumer wine magazine. We pack each of our issues with wine-buying advice based on our exclusive "blind" tastings of wine. Plus, we feature informative articles that stimulate our readers' interests in wine, dining, travel, cooking and collectibles.

This book presents in one convenient pocket-sized package the essential information to understand, buy and enjoy a wide variety of reasonably priced wines from around the world. It includes all the major types of wine that you might look for, from California Chardonnay to French Beaujolais. It can also introduce you to exciting new wines on the scene, like Merlot from Washington state and Sauvignon Blanc from South Africa.

If, like us, you love a bargain almost as much as a great-tasting bottle of wine, this book is for you.

Marvin R. Shanken

Editor and Publisher

Table of Contents

Introduction

USING THIS BOOK TO FIND
GREAT WINE VALUES

BY JIM GORDON

You still don't have to spend a lot of money to buy a really good bottle of wine. In fact, you'll find that the 1997 edition of this up-to-date pocket guide contains even more treasures at $10 a bottle and less.

Interestingly, an even higher proportion of this year's recommendations are American wines. Strong European currencies, poor weather in France and Italy, and American winemaking and marketing savvy combined to place many U.S.—and especially California—wines among the world's best values.

For the purposes of this book, we define a good value as any wine that our editors awarded at least 80 out of 100 points in a *Wine Spectator* tasting, and that has a suggested retail price of $10 or less. In other words, every wine reviewed here carries a solid recommendation. As you begin to use this guide to shop, you will find that wines rated 85 or higher, and those priced as low as $5 or $6, may be the very best values you can find.

The tasting notes and ratings that form the core of this book all come from "blind" wine tastings conducted exclusively by our own editors. By "blind," we mean that the tasters do not know the prices or the wine producers' names when they are tasting and assigning rating points to the wines. This practice is designed to make their reviews as objective as possible.

The reviews published here originate from tastings conducted largely within the 16 months prior to when this book went to press. They are the most current and most specific recommendations you will find in any book of this type. They are designed to help you go shopping.

Following the lead of most wine shops, we grouped the wines by country of origin, then by specific region or grape variety, depending on the custom in that country. For each specific region and type, we list the highest scoring wines on top, to make it easy to know which wines to look for, or ask for, first.

If you take this guide to the wine shop, as we hope you do, use the index in back to quickly find our review for a wine you spot on the shelf. If it's not listed in our guide, it means one of two things: either we reviewed it and it didn't rate high enough to be included, or we didn't review it.

Wine Spectator strives to review all of the widely available wines from important regions that are sold in America. Our total of wines tasted in 1995 will surpass 7,000. Still, it hasn't been possible to review every wine sold in America at $10 or less. The ones you find here, however, are great values.

This guide is as fresh and complete as we could make it. Because new vintages are constantly coming to market, however, we added an extra feature that will give it longer shelf life. For each country, we have created a special list of wines that we know from our tasting experience to be consistent from year to year. These are called "Most Reliable Values." If, for example, you cannot find the vintage we recommend, you can feel safe in buying a more recent vintage from the same company. (Be cautious buying older vintages, however, because most of the wines in this book are meant to be drunk while young and fresh.)

When you turn the page you will find two essays designed to help new wine consumers understand the topic. The first explains how to store and serve wine, and the second has tips for choosing an appropriate wine for a meal.

Following these are the chapters on different wine-producing countries, with specific reviews. Each begins with a brief explanation of that country's important value-oriented wine types, an illustration of how to make sense of its wine labels, and a map showing the major viticultural areas. Each chapter introduction is written by the *Wine Spectator* editor who specializes in wines of that country.

The wine tasting notes and scores, taken together, tell you how much our editors liked the wines, and what styles or flavors you should expect to find. Here's what the ratings mean:

WINE SPECTATOR'S 100-POINT SCALE

95-100: Classic quality, a great wine.

90-94: Outstanding quality, a wine of superior character and style.

80-89: Good to very good quality, a wine with special qualities.

Below 80: Poor to average quality. (Wines that scored below 80 are not included in this book.)

Finally, in response to reader requests, we've added a new feature to the 1997 edition of this book. The symbol ❂ indicates the most widely available wines—those that were produced in quantities of at least 15,000 cases, and thus have the greatest chance of being found on your wine shop's shelves.

Jim Gordon is managing editor of Wine Spectator *magazine.*

Storing and Serving Wine

BY BRUCE SANDERSON

A few basic guidelines in storage and service will go a long way to enhance your enjoyment of wine. The idea is to recognize which of your needs are most important when selecting a wine, its proper serving temperature, and glassware to accommodate the occasion, whether casual or formal.

STORAGE

Once you have purchased wine, whether it's a few bottles or several cases, the issue of storage must be addressed. Since most wine is consumed within 24-48 hours of purchase, for many wine lovers a small rack away from a direct heat source provides an ideal solution. If you plan to collect fine wines that benefit from additional bottle maturation, proper storage is essential. Before choosing a space be sure it will be large enough to accommodate future purchases. In some cases, vacant space beneath a stairway is sufficient, in others it may be necessary to allow for hundreds of wines stored both as individually racked bottles and full cases.

One of wine's greatest enemies is extreme heat. Temperatures greater than 70 degrees Fahrenheit will age a wine more quickly, and can also "cook" a wine until the fruit character becomes blunted, resulting in flat aromas and flavors. Equally important is the rate at which temperature changes. Rapid temperature fluctuations may cause pressure changes within a bottle, forcing the cork upwards and allowing leaks while permitting air to enter the bottle. Air is another of wine's enemies. Any prolonged exposure will lead to oxidation, which produces a brownish color and sherry-like flavors.

Therefore it is important to have a cool space with constant temperature for long-term storage. If your storage area is naturally cool (for example, a below-ground cellar), that's fine; if not, it may be necessary to invest in a cooling unit. Light may also harm wine over time. Bottles should be kept from direct sunlight, preferably in darkness, and should be stored on their sides, either in cases or racked.

Humidity is a more controversial subject but it's nothing to worry about unless you're keeping wines for the long-term. Some experts advocate a constant humidity of 70% to prevent corks from drying out, while others maintain that if a bottle is on its side, the cork is constantly in contact with moisture inside the bottle and external humidity is ineffectual.

SERVING WINES

Most wines may simply be opened and served. Sparkling wines, dessert wines and light-bodied whites need to be chilled to preserve their freshness and fruitiness (34-50 degrees Fahrenheit), while fuller-bodied whites such as Chardonnay and white Rhônes may be served slightly warmer. Light reds (most Beaujolais, Pinot Noir, Cabernet Franc from the Loire valley) benefit from being served slightly cooler than full-bodied reds like Australian Cabernet and Shiraz, California Cabernet and Meritage blends,

Bordeaux and Rhône, which are best at cellar temperature (55-65 degrees Fahrenheit). Of course these are general guidelines and individual tastes may vary.

Most wines are finished with a cork, covered by a capsule of either metal or plastic. To open, cut the capsule around the neck just below the lip of the bottle and remove the top of the capsule. Wipe the top of the bottle with a damp towel or cloth if necessary. Use a corkscrew to remove the cork. There are several different models of corkscrew available; again, the choice is a matter of individual taste.

Champagne and sparkling wines have a different closure, and must be handled carefully since the contents are under pressure and could cause injury. Remove the foil, and with a thumb over the metal crown to prevent the cork from ejecting, loosen the wire fastener. Without removing the wire, grasp the cork firmly and with the other hand turn the bottle, slowly releasing the cork. This process is easier when the wine is well chilled.

In certain instances, it will be necessary to decant a wine. Fine reds with bottle age produce a natural sediment as color pigments and tannins bond together and fall out of solution. Decanting is simply the process of separating the clear wine from the sediment. Before decanting, the bottle should be upright for a minimum 24 hours for the best results. Remove the capsule and cork, and with a light under the neck of the bottle (a candle or flashlight works well), pour the wine into a clean vessel in a single, steady motion until you can see the sediment reach the neck of the bottle. The wine is now ready to serve.

WINE GLASSES

Wine appreciation involves all the senses, and the choice of glassware will influence the sight, aroma, and taste of a wine. Georg Riedel, director of the

Riedel glass company in Austria, has done extensive experimentation using blind tasting trials with professional tasters. He divides glass design into three elements: Clarity and thinness are important for visual perception. The size and shape of the bowl determine the intensity and complexity of the bouquet, and the shape of the rim determines where the wine initially lands on the tongue, affecting the perception of its taste.

White Wine

Clear glass and a thin-rimmed bowl reduce the barriers between the wine lover and the wine. The clearer the glass, the richer the wine's color appears. The thinner the rim, the less the glass distracts from the wine as it enters the mouth. The stem should be long enough so that the hand doesn't touch the bowl, obscuring the glass with fingerprints or warming the wine above proper serving temperature. If the stem is too long, however, the glass will tip too easily. The stem should be about as long as the bowl is tall.

A large bowl and a narrow opening work together to magnify the

Red Wine   **Port**

ILLUSTRATIONS BY HARRY AUNG

Champagne

wine's bouquet. They give plenty of space for the aromas to expand, but only a narrow escape. If the bowl's widest point is too high or too low, a normal serving of wine won't have the maximum surface area for aeration. If the opening is too small, drinking will be difficult.

Many glasses are too small; few are too large. Our evaluations suggest that a good red-wine glass will have a capacity of at least 12 ounces. Generally, glasses for red table wines are wider than those for white, but beyond that it's really up to your personal preference.

Champagne flutes should hold 6 1/2 ounces or more. Sherry and Port glasses traditionally are small, because Port and sherry are fortified wines, and usually drunk in small quantities.

With the exception of sparkling wines, it's best not to fill a wine glass more than half full. This will leave enough air space to release the aromas. Most importantly, find a balance of wine-friendliness, aesthetic appeal and price, and settle on the glass that seems best for you.

Bruce Sanderson is Wine Spectator's *tasting director.*

Matching Wine With Food

By Harvey Steiman

The first thing to remember about matching food and wine is to forget the rules. Forget about shoulds and shouldn'ts. Forget about complicated systems for selecting the right wine with the food on the table. This is not rocket science. It's common sense. Follow your instincts.

The most important rule is to choose a wine that you want to drink by itself. Despite all the hoopla about matching wine and food, you will probably drink most of the wine without the benefit of food— either before the food is served or after you've finished your meal. Therefore, you will not go too far wrong if you make sure the food is good and the wine is, too. Even if the match is not perfect, you will still have an enjoyable wine to drink.

Some of today's food-and-wine pontificators suggest that mediocre wines can be improved by serving them with the right food. The flaw in that reasoning, however, is the scenario described above. If the match does not quite work as well as you hope, you're stuck with a mediocre wine. So don't try to get too fancy. First pick a good wine.

As for which (good) wine to choose, that's where common sense comes in. The old rule about white wine with fish and red wine with meat made perfect sense in the days when white wines were light and fruity and red wines were tannic and weighty. But today, when most California Chardonnays are heavier and fuller-bodied than most California Pinot Noirs, and even some Cabernets, color coding does not always work.

Red wines as a category are distinct from whites in two main ways: tannins—many red wines have them, few white wines do—and flavors. White and red wines share many common flavors; both can be spicy, buttery, leathery, earthy or floral. But the apple, pear and citrus flavors in many white wines seldom show up in reds, and the currant, cherry and stone fruit flavors of red grapes usually do not appear in whites.

In the wine-and-food matching game, these flavor differences come under the heading of subtleties. You can make better wine choices by focusing on a wine's size and weight. Like human beings, wines come in all dimensions. To match them with food, it's useful to know where they fit in a spectrum, with the lightest wines at one end and fuller-bodied wines toward the other end.

A SPECTRUM OF WINES

To help put the world of wines into perspective, consult the following lists, which arrange many of the most commonly encountered wines into a hierarchy based on size, from lightest to weightiest. If you balance the wine with the food by choosing one that will seem about the same weight as the food, you raise the odds dramatically that the match will succeed.

Yes, purists, some Champagnes are more delicate than some Rieslings and some Sauvignon Blancs are bigger than some Chardonnays, but we're trying to paint with broad strokes here. When you're searching for a lightish wine to go with dinner, pick one from the top end of the list. When you want a bigger wine, look toward the end.

SELECTED DRY AND OFF-DRY WHITE WINES, LIGHTEST TO WEIGHTIEST:

Soave and Orvieto
Riesling
Muscadet
Champagne and other dry sparkling wines
Chenin Blanc
French Chablis and other unoaked Chardonnays
Sauvignon Blanc
White Bordeaux
Mâcon
Gewürztraminer
Barrel-fermented or barrel-aged Chardonnay

SELECTED RED WINES, LIGHTEST TO WEIGHTIEST:

Beaujolais
Valpolicella
Dolcetto
Rioja
Burgundy and Pinot Noir
Barbera
Chianti Classico
Merlot
Bordeaux
Zinfandel
Cabernet Sauvignon (U.S., Australian)
Rhône and Syrah

MORE COMMON SENSE

Hearty food needs a hearty wine, because it will make a lighter wine taste insipid. With lighter food, you have more leeway. Lighter wines will balance nicely, of course, but heartier wines will still show you all they have. Purists may complain that full-bodied wines "overwhelm" less hearty foods, but the truth is that anything but the blandest food still tastes fine after a sip of a heavyweight wine.

These are the secrets behind some of the classic wine-and-food matches. Muscadet washes down a plate of oysters because it's just weighty enough to match the delicacy of a raw bivalve. Cabernet complements lamb chops or roast lamb because they're equally vigorous. Pinot Noir or Burgundy makes a better match with roast beef because the richness of texture is the same in both.

To make your own classic matches, follow the same path as the first person who tried Muscadet with oysters. Try a dry Champagne or a dry Riesling, which are on either side of Muscadet on our weight list, for a similar effect. Don't get stuck on Cabernet with lamb. Try Zinfandel or Côtes du Rhône. Instead of Burgundy or Pinot Noir with roast beef, try a little St.-Emilion or Barbera. That's the way to put a little variety into your wine life without straying too far from the original purpose.

At this point, let us interject a few words about sweetness. Some wine drinkers recoil at the thought of drinking an off-dry wine with dinner, insisting that any hint of sweetness in a wine destroys its ability to complement food. In practice, nothing can be further from the truth. How many Americans drink sweetened iced tea with dinner? Lemonade? Or sugary soft drinks? Why should wine be different? The secret is balance. So long as a wine balances its sugar with

enough natural acidity, a match can work. This opens
plenty of avenues for fans of German Rieslings,
Vouvrays and White Zinfandel.

One of the classic wine-and-food matches is
Sauternes, a sweet dessert wine, with *foie gras*—
which blows the sugarphobes' theory completely. The
match works because the wine builds richness upon
richness. The moral of the story is not to let some
arbitrary rules spoil your fun. If you like a wine, drink
it with food you like, and you're bound to be satisfied.

Harvey Steiman is editor-at-large of Wine Spectator.

Australia

By Harvey Steiman

Two factors have contributed to the eye-opening percentage of good values from Australia. One, the Australian dollar is in even worse shape than the U.S. dollar, and two, the wine industry there has worked hard to satisfy a market of Aussies who like to drink wine and prefer to spend as little as possible on it.

The past decade has seen an explosion of interest in Australia for wines that Americans like, too: Chardonnay and Cabernet Sauvignon. These two types, plus Australia's red wine specialty, Shiraz, make up the bulk of Down Under exports to the United States. Riesling is big in Australia itself, where it has long been the quaffing white wine of choice, but few producers bother to export the stuff in this direction.

Australia, like America, labels its best wines with varietal names. The rules are similar, in that varietal wines are made entirely or mostly from the single grape variety named on the front label. Often, more than one variety is named, in which case Shiraz-Cabernet has more Shiraz in it and Cabernet-Shiraz has more Cabernet.

As is true anywhere else, the narrower and more prestigious the geographical appellation, the higher the price of the wine. As a result, most value-oriented wines carry broad appellations, such as Southeastern

Australia—which encompasses a region nearly 600 miles wide—or simply Australia.

Australian vineyards tend to produce grapes with prominent fruit flavors that bring a certain charm even to lesser wines. Aussie winemakers are also brilliant at blending wines from various regions and giving them judicious cellar treatments to achieve a consistent style. Chardonnays such as Lindemans Bin 65 and Oxford Landing from Yalumba are perennial Best Buys in *Wine Spectator* for precisely these reasons.

Other than Chardonnay, Sémillon is the white variety Aussies prize most for the herbal, tobacco and lanolin flavors that sneak in around the fruit. At lower prices, however, we go for Sémillon blended with either Sauvignon Blanc or Chardonnay. The few Rieslings that make it over the Pacific are worth trying, too.

Among the reds, the best values are often Cabernet-Shiraz blends, which tend to carry lower prices than either varietal sold separately. Australian Shirazes in the under-$10 range tend to spill over with delicious fruit. The Cabernets edge toward supple drinkability as well. The blends, though less distinctive, are usually sturdy wines which are drinkable when young.

Finally, don't miss the dessert wines. Australia makes some of the best in the world, including Tawny Ports that live up very well to the Portuguese bottlings they are modeled after, at a fraction of the price. The fortified Muscats may not be fashionable, but they are delicious.

No summary of Australia's best values would be complete without a nod in the direction of Tyrrell's Long Flat White, a consistent Best Buy from a longtime Hunter Valley winery.

Harvey Steiman is editor at large of Wine Spectator.

Most Reliable Values

These wines have proven to be of consistently good quality, year in and year out. Even if a particular vintage is not reviewed here, you may purchase these wines with confidence.

RED WINES

Lindemans Cabernet Sauvignon Bin 45

Rosemount Cabernet Sauvignon

Lindemans Shiraz Bin 50

Rosemount Shiraz

Seppelt Shiraz Reserve Bin

Penfolds Cabernet-Shiraz Koonunga Hill

Rosemount Shiraz-Cabernet

WHITE WINES

Lindemans Chardonnay Bin 65

Penfolds Chardonnay South Australia

Rosemount Sémillion-Chardonnay

Tyrrell's Long Flat White

How to Read an Australian Wine Label

Producer or Estate

Vintage

Proprietary Name

Region of Origin

Grape Variety

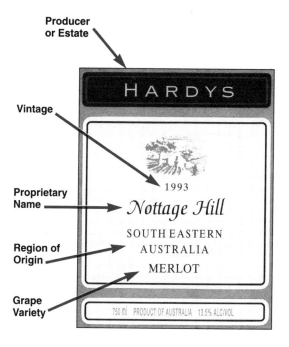

HARDYS

1993

Nottage Hill

SOUTH EASTERN
AUSTRALIA

MERLOT

750 ml   PRODUCT OF AUSTRALIA   13.5% ALC/VOL

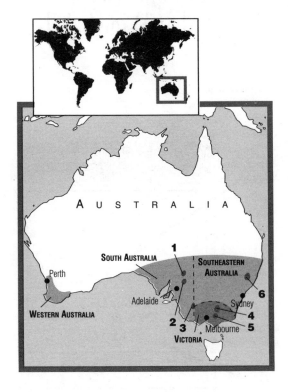

1. Clare   **4.** Goulburn Valley

2. Barossa Valley   **5.** Yarra Valley

3. Coonawarra   **6.** Hunter Valley

RED

Cabernet Blend

86 HARDY'S Cabernet-Shiraz South Eastern Australia Nottage Hill 1994 **$7.00** Crisp and lively, the zingy, herbal currant and cedar flavors jumping through the finish. Approachable now; best in 1998.

86 CHATEAU REYNELLA Cabernet Merlot Basket Pressed McLaren Vale 1993 **$10.00** Chewy but supple and flavorful, with nice berry and spice notes. Better in 1997.

85 OXFORD LANDING Cabernet Sauvignon-Shiraz South Eastern Australia 1993 **$7.00** Light, lean, silky and spicy, with an herbal, tobaccolike character pushing through the chocolaty black cherry flavors—a lot of depth for the money. Try now. ○

84 COCKATOO RIDGE Cabernet Merlot South Eastern Australia 1993 **$7.00** Soft and generous, showing straightforward blackberry and plum flavor that lingers gently on the finish. Drink now.

84 TYRRELL'S Cabernet Merlot South Eastern Australia Old Winery 1994 **$8.00** A nice mouthful of plum and black cherry flavors accompanied by a streak of spicy oak to jazz it up. ○

83 BLACK OPAL Cabernet-Merlot South Eastern Australia 1994 **$9.00** Earthy forest-floor, pickle-barrel notes pop up first, offering just enough blackberry to strike a balance on the finish. Seems too tough and acidic for the flavor profile. Try in 2000 or 2001.

○ = Widest availability (over 15,000 cases produced)

83 QUEEN ADELAIDE Shiraz-Cabernet South Eastern Australia 1993 **$6.00** Light, fruity and easy to drink, adding a streak of gamy Shiraz character to increase the depth. Ready now.

82 COCKATOO RIDGE Cabernet Blend South Eastern Australia 1994 **$9.00** Light and silky, offering a nice range of currant, herb and spice flavors that echo gently on the finish.

82 ORLANDO Shiraz Cabernet South Eastern Australia Jacob's Creek 1994 **$7.00** Smooth and lively, harmonious despite its youth, finishing a little narrow but spicy and fresh. Drinkable now.

82 WOODLEY Shiraz-Cabernet South Eastern Australia Queen Adelaide 1992 **$6.00** Ripe in flavor, crisp in texture and tightly wound; should be at its best in 1997.

80 MITCHELTON Cabernet Sauvignon-Shiraz-Cabernet Franc South Eastern Australia Thomas Mitchell 1994 **$10.00** Light and crisp, showing sour candy overtones to the light, citrusy berry flavors. Ready now.

Cabernet Sauvignon

88 HOUGHTON Cabernet Sauvignon Western Australia Wildflower Ridge 1992 **$8.00** Ripe and generous, offering a lively mouthful of plum, blackberry and a touch of herb and chocolate—all that for a good price. Approachable now, but better from 1997 through 1998.

85 BARRIER REEF Cabernet Sauvignon South Eastern Australia 1992 **$8.00** Light and supple, offering straightforward blackberry and vanilla flavors that maintain spiciness on the finish. Drinkable now.

85 BLACK OPAL Cabernet Sauvignon South Eastern Australia 1994 **$9.00** Crisp and fruity, nicely balanced to show off its strawberry and currant flavors without a load of tannins. Drinkable now, but better in 1997.

85 LINDEMANS Cabernet Sauvignon South Australia Bin 45 1994 **$7.00** Smooth and generous on a modest scale, appealing for its ripe currant, mint and spice flavors. Approachable now; best in 1998. ○

85 MILBURN PARK Cabernet Sauvignon Victoria 1994 **$9.00** Ripe and focused on currant and berry flavors draped over a supple frame that lets the fruit echo on the finish. Approachable now. ○

85 SEAVIEW Cabernet Sauvignon McLaren Vale 1993 **$8.00** Crisp and focused, a tight, lighter style of Cabernet that shows some ripe black cherry flavors.

84 DRAYTON'S Cabernet Sauvignon Hunter Valley 1993 **$10.00** Firm and focused, weaving a nice strand of spice and smoke through the straight-forward currant and plum flavors. Drink now.

84 ROSEMOUNT Cabernet Sauvignon South Australia 1994 **$10.00** Wild, herbal flavors run through the exuberant berry notes in this smooth-textured red. Drinkable now.

84 ROTHBURY Cabernet Sauvignon South Eastern Australia 1994 **$9.00** Crisp in texture, with a minty edge to the light currant flavor, though finishing with a bit more tannin than the wine deserves. Best in 1998. ✪

83 MCWILLIAM'S ESTATE Cabernet Sauvignon South Eastern Australia 1994 **$7.00** Light in texture, as appealingly spicy strawberry and vanilla flavors linger gently on the finish. Drinkable now.

83 SEAVIEW Cabernet Sauvignon South Australia 1992 **$7.50** Surprisingly tough, tannic and somewhat wild, adding a dusky, wild herb edge to the red currant and beetroot flavors. Needs until 1998.

82 KINGSTON ESTATE Cabernet Sauvignon Riverland 1992 **$10.00** Light and polished, a simple wine with appealing but modest red plum, cedar and cherry flavors.

82 SEPPELT Cabernet Sauvignon South Australia Reserve Bin 1993 **$8.00** Light and lean but it shows attractive red berry and vanilla flavors and a crisp finish. Ready now.

80 SEPPELT Cabernet Sauvignon South Australia Black Label 1993 **$10.00** Lean and tough, chewy for the level of fruit which barely peeks through.

Merlot

87 HUNTER RIDGE Merlot South Eastern Australia Vanessa's Vale 1995 **$9.00** Has a nice floral quality in its spicy blueberry and plum flavors. This is light, but it builds up intensity on the modestly tannic finish. Better in 1997.

85 HARDY'S Merlot South Eastern Australia Nottage Hill 1994 **$8.00** Lean, dark and chewy—showing more tannin than fruit right now—but plummy, spicy flavors emerge on the finish. Try in 1998.

85 MCGUIGAN BROTHERS Merlot South Eastern Australia Bin 3000 1995 **$8.00** Light and refreshing, sporting a tropical fruit punch character that lingers appealingly on the bright finish. Drinkable now.

85 OXFORD LANDING Merlot South Eastern Australia 1993 **$7.00** Supple, generous and spicy, showing a chocolaty edge to the black cherry flavors. At a good price and drinkable now.

84 KINGSTON ESTATE Merlot Riverland 1993 **$10.00** Sturdy wine with simple blackberry and toast flavors, finishing with a nice polish. Ready now.

82 LINDEMANS Merlot South Australia Bin 40 1994 **$7.00** Broad but still unfocused; a mouthful of tar and berry flavors are just starting to come together. Try in 1997. ✪

80 ORLANDO Merlot South Eastern Australia Jacob's Creek 1994 **$7.00** Crisp and modestly flavorful, fresh with black cherry and spice flavors.

Shiraz and Shiraz Blend

90 ROSEMOUNT Shiraz South Australia 1994 **$10.00** A ripe, supple and silky Shiraz that is generous with its berry, spice and tar flavors, which also linger enticingly on the finish. Drinkable now. ✪

88 PETER LEHMANN Shiraz Barossa 1993 **$10.00** Brilliantly fruity, as impressive black cherry and pepper flavors keep spilling over on the zippy finish. Approachable now, but best in 1998.

87 BLEASDALE Shiraz-Cabernet Sauvignon Langhorne Creek 1992 **$8.00** Tight and spicy, a lively mouthful of peppery, slightly minty berry flavor. Drinkable now.

87 BLEASDALE Shiraz Langhorne Creek 1993 **$8.00** Firm, focused and lively with peppery plum flavors that linger nicely through the modestly tannic finish. Give it until 1998.

87 SEPPELT Shiraz Victoria Black Label 1992 **$10.00** Ripe and expansive, playing out its spicy plum and black cherry flavors against a touch of tar and tobacco. Delicious now; best in 1997.

87 TYRRELL'S Shiraz Hunter Valley Stevens 1994 **$10.00** Bright and fruity, packed with plum and blueberry flavors on a tightly focused frame. Juicy finish. Drinkable now.

86 KINGSTON ESTATE Shiraz Riverland 1993 **$10.00** Ripe and smooth, a youthful wine with appealing berry and spice flavors. Ready now.

86 LEASINGHAM Shiraz Clare Valley Domaine 1993 **$9.00** Ripe and supple, featuring focused red cherry, berry and spice flavors. Mildly chewy tannins can use until around 1998.

86 LINDEMANS Shiraz South Australia Bin 50 1994 **$8.00** Smooth-textured, with ripe raspberry and cherry flavors and peppery, earthy grace notes on the finish. Drinkable now. ✪

86 CHATEAU REYNELLA Shiraz McLaren Vale Basket Pressed 1993 **$10.00** Firm and chewy, a fountain of generous plum, berry and spice flavors erupting behind a curtain of tannin. Needs until 1998 to soften the tannins, but the fruit is already appealing.

86 ROSEMOUNT Shiraz-Cabernet Australia 1995 **$10.00** A light, bright and fruity red with fresh blackberry flavors. It's appealing to drink now, and priced right. ✪

86 SEAVIEW Shiraz McLaren Vale 1992 **$7.50** Ripe, almost sweet with its plum, spice and blackberry flavors that swirl gently through the lean finish. Drinkable now.

86 TYRRELL'S Shiraz Hunter Valley Old Winery Premier Selection 1993 **$8.00** Lean and lively bright berry and black cherry flavors, zingy, citrusy acidity and a crisp finish.

86 YALUMBA Shiraz Barossa Valley Family Reserve 1993 **$10.00** Focused and flavorful, although it veers off toward an earthy-gamy style, picking up a nice touch of plum on the finish. Best from 1998.

85 HOUGHTON Shiraz Western Australia Wildflower Ridge 1994 **$8.00** An enjoyable wine whose basic berry flavors have distinct herbal and anise overtones. Drinkable now.

85 HUNTER RIDGE Shiraz South Eastern Australia Vanessa's Vale 1995 **$9.00** Youthful, smooth, polished and effusively fruity, showing lots of nice raspberry and red plum flavors that linger on the simple finish. Ready now.

85 MCGUIGAN BROTHERS Black Shiraz South Eastern Australia 1994 **$7.00** Soft and appealing for its straightforward fruit flavors, swirling with blackberry, currant and cranberry flavors, almost sweet on the finish. ✪

85 PENFOLDS Shiraz-Cabernet Sauvignon Australia Koonunga Hill 1994 **$9.00** A little shy on the nose but blackberry flavors come through against the chewy, firm-textured background. Best in 1998.

85 ROTHBURY Shiraz South Eastern Australia 1993 **$8.00** A sturdy style, with gamy overtones to the delicate black cherry and spice flavors. A value-priced red that's drinkable now. ✪

85 SEAVIEW Shiraz McLaren Vale 1993 **$8.00** Lean and a little sharp at the edges, packaging its gamy black cherry flavors in a polished texture. Best from 1998.

84 DRAYTON'S Shiraz South Eastern Australia S5 1995 **$7.50** Bright and ripe, delivering pretty plum and spice flavors on a thin layer of fine tannins, narrowing somewhat on the finish. Best in 1997.

84 HOUGHTON Shiraz Western Australia Wildflower Ridge 1993 **$8.00** Ripe, round and generous, satiny in texture, spicy and plummy in flavor.

84 LINDEMANS Shiraz South Australia Bin 50 1993 **$7.00** Smooth and ripe, medium in weight, featuring appealing plum, spice and tar flavors that soften on the finish. Drink now.

83 ASHWOOD GROVE Shiraz Riverland 1993 **$9.00** Firm and somewhat chewy, offering a nice core of red cherry and berry flavor. Finishes slightly tannic. Best in 1998.

83 MITCHELTON Shiraz South Eastern Australia Thomas Mitchell 1994 **$10.00** Simple and bright, a little coarse in texture but pleasant for its berry and anise flavors.

83 SEPPELT Shiraz South Eastern Australia Reserve Bin 1993 **$8.00** Light, smooth and plummy, lean, adding spicy overtones. Best in 1997.

82 BLACK OPAL Shiraz South Eastern Australia 1994 **$9.00** Firm and a little chewy, somewhat shy on the nose but showing pretty plum and floral flavors as aftertaste. Best in 1998.

82 DRAYTON'S Shiraz Hunter Valley S5 1994 **$7.00** Smooth, gamy, generous tar, animal and berry flavors. Drink now. ✪

82 HARDY'S Shiraz South Eastern Australia Nottage Hill 1993 **$7.00** Smooth and minty, marked by oak, but sneaking some ripe berry and chocolate notes into the finish. Best from 1997.

82 WYNDHAM Shiraz South Eastern Australia Bin 555 1993 **$8.00** Light, smooth and appealing for its smoky strawberry flavors. Not a classically styled Shiraz, but makes a pretty red for immediate enjoyment. ✪

81 MCWILLIAM'S ESTATE Shiraz South Eastern Australia 1994 **$7.00** Light and lean, offering basic berry flavor and a touch of pepper.

Other Red

86 ST. HALLETT Gamekeeper's Reserve Barossa 1994 **$10.00** Smooth and silky, a generous mouthful of minty raspberry, red cherry and plum flavors, finishing polished and lively. Drinkable now.

85 WYNDHAM Pinot Noir South Eastern Australia Bin 333 1994 **$7.00** Starts off with lovely plum and berry fruit, picking up a bass note of earthy, barnyardy flavor on the smooth finish. A distinctive style. ✪

84 TYRRELL'S Pinot Noir Hunter Valley Old Winery 1995 **$7.50** Crisp and lively, sporting juicy, berry flavors on a lean frame. Best in 1997.

83 KINGSTON ESTATE Mourvèdre Riverland 1993 **$10.00** A little chunky at first, but it turns smooth as the blackberry flavor comes through. Ready now.

80 BLEASDALE Malbec Langhorne Creek 1992 **$8.00** Ripe and gamy flavors compete for attention in this light-textured, full flavored wine.

WHITE

Chardonnay

89 ROSEMOUNT Chardonnay Hunter Valley 1995 **$10.00** Ripe, spicy and vibrant apple, pear and citrus flavors whirl and eddy on the zingy finish. A fruit-centered Australian white that has class and depth. ✪

88 HUNTER RIDGE Chardonnay South Eastern Australia Vanessa's Vale 1995 **$9.00** Bright, youthful, focused and appealing for its nectarine, pear and citrus flavor that remains lively through the long finish. Delicious now.

88 MILBURN PARK Chardonnay Victoria 1994 **$9.00** An exuberant mouthful of citrusy pineapple, remaining broad and flavorful through the generous finish. ✪

88 PENFOLDS Chardonnay Australia Koonunga Hill 1995 **$9.00** Light and refreshing, shading its bright nectarine and passion fruit flavors with a touch of citrus. Tangy; bracing to drink now. ✪

88 CHATEAU REYNELLA Chardonnay McLaren Vale 1994 **$10.00** Smooth and spicy, lean at first, but the citrusy, honeyed pear flavors open out on the finish.

88 TYRRELL'S Chardonnay Hunter Valley Shee-Oak Individual Vineyard Non-Wooded 1995 **$10.00** Very spicy, nutty tones in a silky, lightly citrusy white. Harmonious and ultimately elegant. Has plenty of flavor and character. Drinkable now.

87 COWRA ESTATE Chardonnay 1992 **$10.00**
Bright, lively and appealing for its lingering green
apple, vanilla and spice flavors.

87 SEPPELT Chardonnay South Australia Black
Label 1994 **$10.00** Ripe and spicy, broad enough to
support a range of resiny pear and citrusy flavors.
Drinkable now.

87 TYRRELL'S Chardonnay South Eastern
Australia Old Winery Premier Selection 1995
$7.50 Fresh and fruity, featuring soft nectarine and
vanilla flavors that spread out gently on the finish.
Drinkable now. ✪

85 BARRIER REEF Chardonnay South Eastern
Australia 1993 **$8.00** Ripe, broad and generous with
its pear and pineapple notes, finishing supple and a
little spicy.

85 DRAYTON'S Chardonnay Hunter Valley
1995 **$9.00** Bright and grapy, with a resiny edge to
the exuberant fruit flavors that form up into a nicely
focused line on the finish. Ready now.

85 DRAYTON'S Chardonnay South Eastern
Australia 1995 **$9.00** Ripe and generous, appealing
for its spicy pear and nectarine flavors.

85 ROTHBURY Chardonnay Hunter Valley 1995
$8.00 Bright and steely, with a nice bead of fresh
apple and pear flavors zinging through it. ✪

84 HARDY'S Chardonnay South Eastern
Australia Nottage Hill 1995 **$7.00** Simple, fresh
and lively, appealing for its citrusy peach character.
Enjoy soon. ✪

84 MCWILLIAM'S ESTATE Chardonnay South Eastern Australia 1995 **$7.00** Light, fruity and refreshing, showing pleasant nectarine and citrus flavors. Drinkable now.

84 OXFORD LANDING Chardonnay South Eastern Australia 1995 **$8.00** Crisp at first, with a nice layer of creaminess on the light finish. Ready now. ✪

84 PENFOLDS Chardonnay South Australia 1994 **$9.00** Broad and flavorful, a bit medicinal but rich and spicy on the finish. Ready now.

84 REDBANK Chardonnay South Eastern Australia Long Paddock 1994 **$10.00** Soft, ripe and generous with its nectarine and spice flavors. Drinkable now.

84 DAVID WYNN Chardonnay South Eastern Australia 1994 **$10.00** Light and spicy, offering enough fruit to keep it charming, persisting on the finish.

83 BLACK OPAL Chardonnay South Eastern Australia 1995 **$9.00** Smooth and creamy, soft, offering pleasant peach flavors. Drinkable now.

83 LINDEMANS Chardonnay South Eastern Australia Bin 65 1995 **$7.00** A light, crisp, simple wine, but with pleasant pineapple and spice flavors that linger nicely on the finish. ✪

83 SEAVIEW Chardonnay McLaren Vale 1995 **$8.00** Bright and citrusy, flavors centered around orange and vanilla. Ready now.

82 COCKATOO RIDGE Chardonnay South Eastern Australia 1994 **$9.00** Light and lively, with lots of bright fruit and spice flavors.

81 DRAYTON'S Chardonnay South Eastern Australia C6 1995 **$8.00** Soft and maybe a bit sweet, showing some nice apricot, pear and honey flavors that remain zesty on the finish.

81 ORLANDO Chardonnay South Eastern Australia Jacob's Creek 1995 **$7.00** The bright yellow color is odd, but the fresh apple and pineapple flavors are appealing. Drinkable now. ○

81 QUEEN ADELAIDE Chardonnay South Eastern Australia 1994 **$6.00** Fresh and light, showing pleasant appley and grassy flavors.

81 SEPPELT Chardonnay South Eastern Australia Reserve Bin 1994 **$8.00** Lean and lively, showing more crisp texture than flavor for now. Try now. ○

80 CEDAR CREEK Chardonnay South Eastern Australia Bin 33 1995 **$7.00** Light and appealing, with simple citrusy flavors. Ready now. ○

Sauvignon Blanc

90 TALTARNI Sauvignon Blanc Victoria 1995 **$10.00** Very fresh and spicy, packed with nectarine and vanilla flavors that linger enticingly on the finish. Big and refreshing at the same time. Drinkable now.

85 MILBURN PARK Sauvignon Blanc Victoria 1994 **$8.00** Light and satiny, with pleasant orange peel and grapefruit notes to keep it lively.

84 ROSEMOUNT Fumé Blanc Hunter Valley 1994 **$10.00** Soft and supple, featuring a green apple-herbal streak cutting through the spicy freshness. Lingering finish.

84 SEAVIEW Sauvignon Blanc McLaren Vale 1994 **$9.00** Lean and spicy, with a snappy shot of pure fruit and an interesting overlay of sweet pea character. ○

83 BARRIER REEF Sauvignon Blanc South Eastern Australia 1993 **$7.00** Ripe and spicy, vanilla-oak flavors weaving through the green apple and spice.

80 OXFORD LANDING Sauvignon Blanc South Eastern Australia 1994 **$7.00** Soft and spicy, layering some butterscotch over the modest pear and spice flavors. Ready now.

Sémillon and Sémillon Blend

87 PENFOLDS Sémillon-Chardonnay South Australia Koonunga Hill 1995 **$8.00** Bright, fruity, lively peach and pear flavors linger on the finish, echoing toast and fruit. Drinkable now. ○

86 HANWOOD Sémillon-Chardonnay Australia 1993 **$6.00** Nicely focused pear, fig and tobacco flavors give this soft, appealing wine a classic feel. Attractive both for its character and its price.

85 DRAYTON'S Sémillon Hunter Valley 1993 **$8.00** Broad and distinctive, featuring lanolin over-tones to the pear and tobacco flavors. Ready now, but should improve through 1997.

85 DRAYTON'S Sémillon-Chardonnay Hunter Valley Oakey Creek 1994 **$7.00** Fruity, supple and charming. Appealing for its green apple and spice flavors.

85 SEAVIEW Sémillon Sauvignon Blanc McLaren Vale 1994 **$9.00** Bright, fresh and flavorful. A floral- and tobacco-scented white that follows through with a lovely mouthful of pear and spice flavors. ✪

85 WYNDHAM Sémillon-Chardonnay South Eastern Australia Bin 777 1995 **$6.00** A rich, spicy and fragrant Australian blend that keeps its floral, citrus and green apple flavors bouncing brightly on the finish. A lot of character for only a few bucks. ✪

84 REDBANK Sémillon South Eastern Australia Long Paddock 1994 **$10.00** Broad and distinctive, boasting fig, hay and citrus peel flavors that build up richness on the palate.

83 LINDEMANS Sémillon-Chardonnay South Australia Bin 77 1995 **$7.00** Fruity flavors center around pineapple, showing oily texture and tart, citrus notes on the finish. A different sort of white. Best in 1997.

83 ROSEMOUNT Sémillon Chardonnay South Eastern Australia 1995 **$8.00** Round and smooth, with pleasant pineapple flavors and an agreeable touch of wool sneaking in on the finish. Maybe better in 1997. ✪

83 DAVID WYNN Sémillon Chardonnay South Eastern Australia 1993 **$9.00** Soft and floral, generous with its gooseberry and apple flavors.

82 SEPPELT Sémillon Chardonnay South Eastern Australia 1994 **$6.00** Has a definite earthy, haylike character that rolls over the other flavors, although it finishes with a nice touch of citrusy acidity.

82 TYRRELL'S Sémillon Chardonnay South Eastern Australia Long Flat 1995 **$6.00** Bright and fresh, with lively citrus and pear flavors and a touch of herb on the finish. ✪

81 CEDAR CREEK Sémillon Blend South Eastern Australia Bin 11 1994 **$6.00** Simple and bright, tasty for its citrusy apple flavors. ✪

80 ORLANDO Sémillon Chardonnay South Eastern Australia Jacob's Creek 1995 **$7.00** Crisp, straightforward and appealing for its soft pear and citrus flavors. ✪

80 SEAVIEW Sémillon Sauvignon Blanc McLaren Vale 1994 **$7.50** Crisp and citrusy, with a touch of onion around the edges.

Other White

87 ROSEMOUNT Traminer-Riesling South Eastern Australia 1995 **$8.00** Spicy, fruity and refreshing, a zingy mouthful of peach, green apple, litchi and spice flavors that remain lively through the finish. Great as an apéritif.

86 DRAYTON'S Verdelho Hunter Valley 1995 **$10.00** Broad and fruity, a mouthful of green apple and citrusy flavors that linger nicely as the finish turns crisp. Ready now.

85 BLEASDALE White Burgundy Langhorne Creek 1995 **$8.00** Simple, bright, broad and fruity, a nice mouthful of peach, pear and spice flavors that persist on the sturdy finish.

84 ST. HALLETT Poacher's Blend Barossa 1995 **$10.00** Tastes remarkably like fruit cocktail, fresh and generous with its pear, grape and melon flavors from beginning to end.

84 TYRRELL'S Long Flat White South Eastern Australia 1995 **$6.00** Soft and fruity, with clean, pleasant grapefruit and tropical fruit flavors that finish light. Drink soon to enjoy its freshness. ✪

83 MITCHELTON Marsanne South Eastern Australia 1995 **$10.00** Lean and crisp, adding a citrusy edge to the peach flavors. Drinkable now.

SPARKLING

86 YALUMBA Brut Australia Angas NV **$10.00** A sparkling wine style that favors creamy, buttery, lightly honeyed flavors, finishing with a touch of pear and spice. Balanced and rich in flavor. ✪

86 YALUMBA Sparkling Australia Angas Brut Rosé NV **$10.00** Fresh and inviting, a lovely mouthful of berry and floral-scented spice and citrus flavors that linger delicately on the finish.

83 CHATEAU REYNELLA Brut Australia NV **$9.00** Dark, toasty, spicy style, a little sweet on the finish, appealing for its floral notes.

DESSERT

89 PENFOLDS Port Australia Club NV **$9.00** Very spicy, sporting caramel, cinnamon and tarry flavors, sweet and silky on the long finish.

89 YALUMBA Tawny Port South Australia Clocktower NV **$10.00** Goes for lightness and elegance and achieves a spicy complexity that's rare in a wine of this price range. Hints of licorice, cinnamon and tar emerge on the smooth finish.

87 TYRRELL'S Tawny Port Australia 8 Barrels NV **$9.00** Spicy and glowing with litchi fruit flavors like Muscat, sweet and touched by caramel notes on the open finish.

Chile

BY THOMAS MATTHEWS

Chile makes wines that Americans like to drink. These wines are fresh and fruity, have straightforward varietal character, and sell for reasonable prices. That's why this small, dynamic wine producer has become the third-largest exporter to the United States, led only by Italy and France.

Simplicity is the key to Chile's success. The wines are made from grapes Americans already know and like: Cabernet Sauvignon and Merlot for the reds, Sauvignon Blanc and Chardonnay for the whites. Vintages hardly matter, because Chile's vineyards enjoy temperate, semi-arid weather conditions that ripen the grapes consistently from year to year. The appellation system is relatively primitive and the big wineries tend to blend fruit from widely-spread grow-ing regions, so regional character is still blurred (though beginning to emerge). Most of the Chilean wines we see in America are produced by a handful of large companies, so labels are few and brands are consistent. It's simply hard to go wrong.

Chile's wine industry was founded in the 1850s by wealthy aristocrats who modeled their estates after the châteaux of Bordeaux. Most of the wineries were established in the Maipo Valley just south of Santiago, Chile's capital. This is still the heart of Chile's wine country, which extends 250 miles through the coun-try's Central Valley, a narrow, fertile plain at the foot of the Andes. Chile's best wines are still made from

Bordeaux's traditional grape varities: Cabernet
Sauvignon, Merlot and Sauvignon Blanc.

The style of Chilean wines tends to resemble the
elegance of Europe rather than the power of the New
World. The reds are the best bets so far. Refreshing,
and a great accompaniment to food, they are polished,
rarely heavy or jammy, and have bright fruit, firm acidity and light tannins. Most are ready to drink two or
three years after harvest; few reward extended cellaring.
The top Cabernets still come from the Maipo Valley,
but look also for Cabs and Merlots from Colchagua, a
sub-region of the Rapel Valley south of Maipo.

The whites have played second fiddle so far.
Chardonnay has only been widely planted for about
ten years, and though good examples are available, it
lacks the overall consistency and character of the other
varietal wines, mostly offering straightforward fruit
with some oak influence. Sauvignon Blanc is more
exciting, especially wines coming from the newest
vineyard region, Casablanca; crisp and exuberant, they
mix fruit and herb flavors in refreshing balance.

Chilean wines vary in price from under $5 per
bottle to nearly $15, and overall you get what you pay
for. Because the soil is fertile and irrigation permitted
and often overused, the vines can be made to yield
enormous harvests; the result can be simple wines
with little concentration or varietal character at the
low end of the price range. But the top wineries are
seeking out better matches of site and grape variety,
reducing yields and improving their vinification meth-
ods, with the result that wines in the $8 to $12 range
are better now than ever. (Chile's more expensive pres-
tige wines, unfortunately, are sometimes over-ambi-
tious, suffering from overoaking and overextraction.)

Today, Chile's top wineries offer clean, accessible
wines in food-friendly styles at reasonable prices,
which are likely to remain attractive bargains to

Most Reliable Values

These wines have proven to be of consistently good quality, year in and year out. Even if a particular vintage is not reviewed here, you may purchase these wines with confidence.

Red Wines

Alameda Maipo Valley Santa Maria Vineyard Merlot

Alameda Maipo Valley Vintner's Selection
   Cabernet Sauvignon

Canepa Curicó Cabernet Sauvignon-Malbec

Carmen Maule Valley Merlot

Casa Lapostolle Colchagua Cabernet Sauvignon

Montes Curicó Special Cuvée Merlot

Santa Rita Maipo Valley Reserve Cabernet
   Sauvignon

White Wines

Santa Rita Maule Valley Chardonnay

Santa Rita Maule Valley 120 Sauvignon Blanc

American wine drinkers. But over the next few years, the top players and emerging boutique wineries will push wine quality higher. Don't be surprised to find outstanding wines, still at fair prices, emerging from Chile before too long.

Thomas Matthews is New York bureau chief of Wine Spectator.

How to Read a Chilean Wine Label

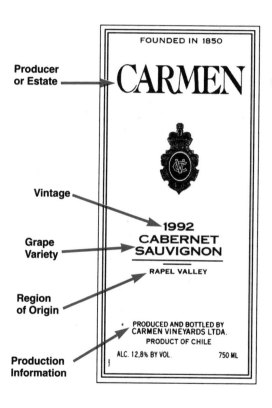

Producer or Estate →

Vintage

Grape Variety

Region of Origin

Production Information

FOUNDED IN 1850

CARMEN

1992
CABERNET
SAUVIGNON

RAPEL VALLEY

PRODUCED AND BOTTLED BY
CARMEN VINEYARDS LTDA.
PRODUCT OF CHILE

ALC. 12,8% BY VOL.   750 ML

1. Aconcagua   4. Rapel
2. Casablanca   5. Colchagua
3. Maipo   6. Maule

RED

Cabernet Sauvignon and Cabernet Blend

88 SANTA AMELIA Cabernet Sauvignon Colchagua 1994 **$6.00** Richer and more structured than most Chilean Cabs, which makes this an especially good value. It offers smoky oak aromas, concentrated plum and black cherry flavors and a lively tobacco note. The tannins are firm, and it's lush and generous. Drinkable now, but may improve through 1997. ✪

87 CASA LAPOSTOLLE Cabernet Sauvignon Colchagua 1994 **$9.00** Attractive tar and smoke aromas give way to plum and smoky flavors and ample tannins. Good sense of polish and varietal flavor. Should improve through 1997.

87 DE MARTINO Cabernet Sauvignon Maipo Valley Prima De Martino Vineyard 1993 **$8.00** Good concentration here. Rich, velvety texture is supported by firm, ripe tannins, giving it intensity, but the coffee and cassis flavors are a bit muted now. Try now.

85 ALAMEDA Cabernet Sauvignon Maipo Valley Vintner's Selection 1993 **$5.00** Fresh, vivid black cherry and chocolate flavors are backed by crisp acidity and firm tannins. Balanced and respectably intense, and shows what Chile does best. ✪

85 CANEPA Cabernet Sauvignon-Malbec Curicó 1994 **$5.00** Round and fruity, this shows good Cabernet character, adding cassis, herbal and smoky flavors and just enough tannin to stand up to food. Balanced and frank.

✪ = Widest availability (over 15,000 cases produced)

85 SANTA RITA Cabernet Sauvignon Maipo Valley Reserva 1993 **$10.00** Dense and muscular for a Chilean red, with a nice balance of ripe plum and toasty oak. It's still firm and closed, but would match well with hearty food.

85 VIU MANENT Cabernet Sauvignon Colchagua Valley Proprietor's Reserve 1991 **$6.00** Initial barnyard aroma is off-putting, but it disappears and ripe, roasted plum and blackberry flavors emerge. Round and velvety, sporting vanilla oak notes on the long finish.

84 CONCHA Y TORO Cabernet Sauvignon Maipo Valley Trio 1994 **$8.00** Appealing chocolate and mint aromas give way to ripe, fleshy flavors of plum, mint and toast. The tannins are supple but add some backbone to the lush palate. Drinkable now.

84 DE MARTINO Cabernet Sauvignon Maipo Valley De Martino Vineyard 1994 **$5.00** Bright cherry, herbaceous and bell pepper notes say Cabernet, offering fresh acidity and just enough backbone for balance. A good food wine for early drinking.

84 LAS CASAS DEL TOQUI Cabernet Sauvignon Cachapoal 1995 **$10.00** Lively, fresh and chunky, with moderate tannins and soft acidity. Leaning toward the herbal, gamy side of Cabernet. Drinkable now.

83 SANTA ALICIA Cabernet Sauvignon Maipo Valley Reserve 1990 **$8.00** Though light-bodied and somewhat tannic, this Cabernet Sauvignon delivers interesting cassis, black pepper and herbal notes that linger on the finish. A good food wine.

83 VIÑA PORTA Cabernet Sauvignon Valle del Cachapoal 1994 **$9.00** Really fruity, with lots of straightforward cherry and berry flavors, modest tannins and a crisp bite on the finish. Should continue to mellow.

83 VIÑA SEGÚ OLLÉ Cabernet Sauvignon Maule Valley Doña Consuelo Reserve 1993 **$8.00** Fresh and clean, with pleasantly brisk tannins, this is varietally correct, though the flavors fall onto the herbal, green bean side, with light cherry accents. Drink now.

82 MONTES Cabernet Sauvignon Curicó Villa Montes 1993 **$7.00** Light, vivid raspberry flavors that burst, then fade. Simple but pleasant. ✪

82 SANTA ALICIA Cabernet Sauvignon Maipo Valley 1990 **$6.00** Cassis and herbal aromas are appealing. The palate is a bit flat but offers plum and licorice flavors backed by modest tannins. Still fresh; best to drink now.

81 ALAMEDA Cabernet Sauvignon Maipo Valley Santa Maria Vineyard 1993 **$6.50** This firm red shows herbal, earthy and gamy flavors. Its rich but could use more fruit. ✪

Merlot

88 SANTA ALICIA Merlot Maipo Valley Reserve 1992 **$8.00** Effusively young and fresh for a '92, with a dollop of blueberry flavors and aromas. Concentrated, ripe and balanced, with a good backbone of tannins. Easy to like and delicious, this bargain from Chile finishes with a hint of mint.

86 ALAMEDA Merlot Maipo Valley Santa Maria Vineyard 1993 **$6.00** This polished Chilean red offers well-balanced flavors of currant, game, black pepper and toast. Drinkable now, but enough structure to improve in the short term. ✪

86 SANTA AMELIA Merlot Colchagua 1994 **$6.00** An easy going Chilean wine that's a good value. Plenty of plum and chocolate flavors; ripe, bold and well balanced, with a touch of herbal character. It finishes with some clovelike flavors. ✪

85 CONCHA Y TORO Merlot Peumo Valley Trio 1995 **$8.00** Lush, fleshy, characteristic blackberry and tomato flavors, supple tannins and a sweet hint of oak. Plenty of fruit for early drinking.

85 MONTES Merlot Curicó Special Cuvée 1994 **$8.00** A stylish, fresh Merlot with deep color, spicy aromas, plum and berry flavors and ample oak accents. Moderately tannic, but smooth enough to drink now through 1997. ✪

85 MONTES Merlot Curicó Villa Montes 1995
$7.00 Fresh and very flavorful, like blackberry jam
without the sweetness. Deep purple in color, peppery
in aroma, smooth and lush in texture. Not tannic, so
it's ready to drink. Good value and enjoyment—what
the Chileans do best. ✪

85 SAN CARLOS Merlot Colchagua Valley 1994
$6.00 A rich, chocolaty Merlot that is fairly soft and
round. Generous and well proportioned, with ripe plum,
cherry and cassis flavors. Finishes with coffee notes.

83 RIVER FALLS Merlot Colchagua 1994 **$6.00**
Hearty, definitely on the herbal and tannic side, but
fairly rich overall. Some ripe plum and cherry flavors
with a touch of bittersweet chocolate on the finish.
Needs to smooth out a little. ✪

82 CARMEN Merlot Maule Valley 1994 **$6.00**
Light and fruity, fresh in flavor and easy to drink.
Reminds us of strawberries. Charming.

82 DE MARTINO Merlot Maipo Valley De
Martino Vineyard 1994 **$6.00** Smoky and herbal
flavors are prominent in this lean, supple Merlot. It's
showing more tannin than fruit.

81 VIÑA SEGÚ OLLÉ Merlot Maule Valley Doña
Consuelo 1995 **$6.00** A smoky-tasting Merlot with
earthy, herbal flavors and moderate tannins.

80 CARMEN Merlot Maule Valley Reserve 1994
$10.00 A tough-textured red of modest fruit flavor
that is good and drinkable, but not as filled out as it
ought to be.

Other Red

86 MONTES Malbec Colchagua 1995 **$8.00** A wine with good varietal character delivering smoky, gamy and pruny flavors, some toasty oak, and enough acidity to maintain liveliness. It's fresh, rich and ready to drink now.

86 SAN CARLOS Malbec Colchagua Valley Oak Aged 1994 **$6.00** Smoky bacon and licorice flavors are typical of Malbec, while the supple fruitiness is characteristic of Chile. An appealing red for drinking now.

WHITE

Chardonnay

86 SANTA ALICIA Chardonnay Maipo Valley Reserve 1993 **$8.00** Vivid and still fresh. Aromas of honey and flowers give way to delicate but lively flavors of tangerine, melon and vanilla. It's harmonious and lingers on the finish.

84 CONCHA Y TORO Chardonnay Casablanca Valley Casillero del Diablo 1994 **$9.00** Smoky, oaky aromas give way to a tight palate that features crisp acidity and fresh melon flavors. Ambitious and full-blown, if a bit awkward.

84 CONCHA Y TORO Chardonnay Casablanca Valley Trio 1995 **$8.00** This lively white has a good balance of crisp acidity and sweet oak, with buttery aromas and tropical fruit flavors. It's fresh and clean, if a bit short.

84 SANTA RITA Chardonnay Maipo Valley Reserva 1995 **$10.00** Vivid and energetic, this light-bodied white is crisp and clean, and offers a nice balance of smoky oak, lime and apple. Good intensity.

83 CARMEN Chardonnay Central Valley 1995 **$6.00** A smooth, polished wine with a nice balance of oak and fruit. Discreet flavors of apples and pears lead to a slightly herbal finish. Good with food.

83 LAS CASAS DEL TOQUI Chardonnay Cachapoal Grande Réserve 1995 **$10.00** Plenty of oak gives this wine rich, toasty, buttery flavors, and there's just enough melon and apple to keep it in balance.

83 SANTA MONICA Chardonnay Rancagua 1995 **$6.50** Full-bodied, if a bit lean in flavor, for a Chilean Chardonnay. Nice apple notes with hints of herb and smoke.

82 SAN CARLOS Chardonnay Colchagua 1995 **$6.00** This snappy white offers light, crisp apple and citrus flavors, fresh and lean. A delightful apéritif.

82 SANTA AMELIA Chardonnay Colchagua 1994 **$6.00** Light and refreshing, this features pleasant apple and beeswax aromas, then turns crisp on the palate, though without much fruit. Clean and likable. ✪

82 SANTA RITA Chardonnay Maule Valley 120 1995 **$6.00** A crisp, straightforward wine. The smoky and green apple flavors are lean, but the overall impression is fresh and clean.

82 VIÑA PORTA Chardonnay Valle del Cachapoal 1995 **$9.00** Full-bodied for Chile, with attractive spicy oak notes. The flavors lean more towards herbal than fruity.

81 CASA LAPOSTOLLE Chardonnay Colchagua Selection 1994 **$9.00** Soft and buttery, gentle and a bit flabby. The delicate melon flavors are pleasant now, but chill it well and drink up.

81 CAVAS DEL RACO Chardonnay Alto Maipo Oak Medley 1990 **$10.00** Not your normal Chardonnay. The honey, spice and candied apple flavors suggest a late-harvest wine, though there's not much sweetness. It's concentrated and distinctive; better alone than with food.

81 DE MARTINO Chardonnay Maipo Valley De Martino Vineyard 1995 **$6.00** Fresh and crisp, featuring enough pear and peach flavors to balance the soft vanilla notes. It's simple but appealing.

Sauvignon Blanc

83 DE MARTINO Sauvignon Blanc Maipo Valley Fumé De Martino Vineyard 1995 **$7.00** Ripe flavors of pineapple and pear are enriched by light vanilla notes in this round white. Though lacking in classic varietal character, it's fresh and clean.

83 SANTA RITA Sauvignon Blanc Maule Valley 120 1995 **$6.00** A snappy wine, with crisp gooseberry flavors, light herbal notes and good acidity. It's fresh and light.

83 VIÑA SEGÚ OLLÉ Sauvignon Blanc Maule Valley Doña Consuelo 1994 **$6.00** Bright pineapple and lime flavors with sweet oak make this a lively white with moderate acidity. Not complex, but vivid enough to pair with food.

82 SAN CARLOS Sauvignon Blanc Colchagua Valley 1994 **$6.00** Round and fleshy for a Sauvignon Blanc, this has ripe pear and herbal flavors and buttery accents. It's soft and full, showing just enough acidity for balance.

81 ALAMEDA Sauvignon Blanc Maipo Valley Vintner's Selection 1994 **$5.00** Ripe and soft flavors of vanilla, butter and melon indicate Chardonnay more than Sauvignon Blanc. Intriguing, but not for everyone. ✪

80 ERRAZURIZ Sauvignon Blanc Maule 1995 **$8.00** Assertive lime and green apple flavors provide a crisp, clean profile. Not rich, but quite refreshing. ✪

80 SANTA RITA Sauvignon Blanc Maule Valley Reserva 1995 **$10.00** The oak dominates the apple flavors in this wine and turns a bit bitter on the finish. Fine for a glass or two; might not stand up to food.

80 UNDURRAGA Sauvignon Blanc Maipo Valley 1995 **$6.00** Lively and straightforward, this simple white offers light citrus and pineapple flavors and a clean finish.

Other White

83 SANTA MONICA Sémillon Rancagua 1994
$5.50 Fresh, lively spice and peach flavors produce
enough vivacity for this white to stand on its own, and
enough weight to stand up to food.

Dessert

81 VIÑA SEGÚ OLLÉ Moscatel de Alejandria
Maule Valley Doña Consuelo 1994 **$6.00** An
exotic wine with a fruit-salad mix of flavors. Orange,
pineapple, honey and nut flavors mingle in this
assertive wine that's pleasant and reminiscent of hard
candy in its simplicity and slightly sweet finish.

France

BY JAMES SUCKLING

When most people think of France, they think of the great and expensive wines from such areas as Bordeaux, Burgundy and the Rhône Valley. However, the French also make a wealth of interesting and reasonably priced wines, from both renowned and little known regions.

All the areas included in the country's rather complex system of wine designations, the *appellation controlée*, produce wines offering good value for the money—even in regions where the top wines cost several hundred dollars per bottle. The key regions to look for include Alsace, Beaujolais, Bordeaux, Burgundy, and the Loire and Rhône Valleys. Most of these regions make wines from different grape varieties, so it's helpful to know what grape variety or region you prefer. For instance, a vintner in Beaujolais makes light and refreshing red wines, which are best consumed young, from Gamay grapes. In Bordeaux, the red wines are made predominantly from Cabernet Sauvignon and Merlot, and are generally better for aging.

A recent trend toward making varietal wines with the name of just one grape variety on the label has made things easier for many people, although most of these wines do not come from areas within the *appellation controlée* system. The majority are produced in the Midi, a huge wine producing area in the southeast of France which encompasses a number of regions including Languedoc-Roussilion and Provence. Wines labeled as Cabernet Sauvignon, Syrah, Chardonnay and Sauvignon Blanc from here all usually carry the designation "Vin de Pays," which loosely translates to "Country Wine."

Regardless of which region or grape variety you choose, it's often best to buy wines by the producer's name—one with a reputation for consistent quality and value. Many of the wines listed in this year's guide are made by producers who, nearly every vintage, make wines which impress us with their high quality and reasonably low prices.

Perhaps the most impressive producer of values is Georges Duboeuf, often called the "King of Beaujolais." From white Burgundy to Syrah from the deep South of France, Duboeuf knows how to select the best wines to be bottled under his label. Two of his Beaujolais, one each from the districts of Chénas and Morgon, tied for the best value wine from France; the Chénas in particular is a giveaway at $8.50 a bottle. If you can't find this wine, try any of the 16 other 1995 Duboeuf Beaujolais in this guide. All are priced between $8 and $10 a bottle.

Fortant de France is another producer that can be relied upon for good value wines, and this fast-growing wine company is leading the new wave of varietal wines from the South of France. Its 1994 Merlot received 83 points and sells for around $7 a bottle.

While these relatively new varietal wines from the Midi get a lot of attention and space in wine shops, the traditional regional wines should not be overlooked. Even Bordeaux, which is best known for its $100-a-bottle red wines, makes a strong showing in the value category. After two fairly dismal vintages in

THE FRENCH MAKE A WEALTH OF INTERESTING AND REASONABLY PRICED WINES, FROM BOTH RENOWNED AND LITTLE KNOWN REGIONS.

1991 and 1992 because of poor weather, the newer wines—both red and white—from 1993, 1994 and soon 1995 are generally better in quality. Choose carefully in this category, however, because an impressive looking label showing a regal chateau often says more about the label designer's skill than the winemaker's.

In the region of Alsace, J.B. Adam is one name to watch for; its wines are some of the best produced in the area—and the most reasonably priced. Adam's '93 Riesling Réserve received the fine score of 88 points, and at $9 a bottle, the price is simply remarkable.

All in all, France continues to offer a bounty of good wines for the money, despite its rather elitist reputation. The biggest difficulty is deciding what to buy.

James Suckling is European bureau chief of Wine Spectator.

Most Reliable Values

These wines have proven to be of consistently good quality, year in and year out. Even if a particular vintage is not reviewed here, you may purchase these wines with confidence.

BEAUJOLAIS

George Duboeuf Beaujolais-Villages Flower Label

George Duboeuf Brouilly Flower Label

George Duboeuf Morgon Flower Label

Louis Jadot Beaujolais-Villages

Mommessin Beaujolais-Villages

BORDEAUX RED

Château Bonnet Bordeaux Reserve

Château Bonnet Entre-Deux-Mers Vinifié en
  Fûte Neuf

Chateau Haut-Mazieres

RHÔNE

Paul Jabolet Aîné Côtes du Ventoux

M. Chapoutier Côtes du Rhône Belleruche

Other Red Wines

Baron Philippe de Rothschild Vin de Pays d'Oc
Cabernet Sauvignon

Fortant de France Vin de Pays d'Oc Merlot

Les Jamelles Vin de Pays d'Oc Cabernet Sauvignon

Mommessin Vin de Pays d'Oc Merlot

Sauvion & Fils Muscadet de Sèvre et Maine Sur Lie
Carte Noire

Alsace

Domaines Schlumberger Pinot Blanc

Leon Beyer Pinot Blanc

Pierre Sparr Riesling Carte d'Or

Other White Wines

Baron Philippe de Rothschild Vin de Pays d'Oc
Chardonnay

Château Bonnet Entre-Deux-Mers

Fortant de France Vin de Pays d'Oc Chardonnay

George Duboeuf Vin de Pays d'Oc Chardonnay

Maitre d'Estournel Bordeaux White

Chartron & Trébuchet Bourgogne Chardonnay

Sparkling

Varichon & Clerc Blanc de Blancs

How to Read a French Wine Label: I

Producer or Estate

Region of Origin

Importer

Production Information

How to Read a
French Wine Label: II

**Brand or
Proprietary
Name**

**Grape
Variety**

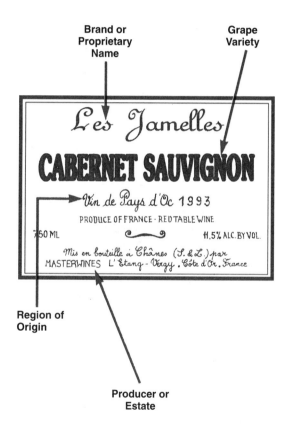

Les Jamelles

CABERNET SAUVIGNON

Vin de Pays d'Oc 1993

PRODUCE OF FRANCE · RED TABLE WINE

750 ML

11.5% ALC. BY VOL.

Mis en bouteille à Chânes (S. & L.) par
MASTERWINES L'Etang - Vergy . Côte d'Or . France

**Region of
Origin**

**Producer or
Estate**

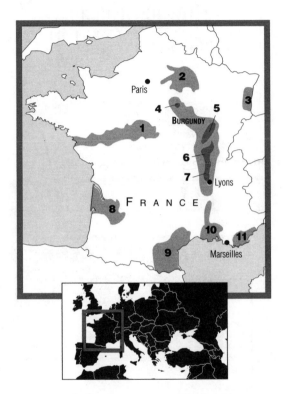

1. Loire
2. Champagne
3. Alsace
4. Chablis
5. Côte d'Or
6. Mâcon
7. Beaujolais
8. Bordeaux
9. Languedoc-Roussillion (d'Oc)
10. Rhône
11. Provence

RED

Beaujolais

88 GEORGES DUBOEUF Chénas Domaine des Darroux 1995 **$8.50** Quite powerful for Beaujolais. This wine is dark in color, with intense plum aromas, and big tannins under ripe plum and cassis flavors. Drinkable now.

88 GEORGES DUBOEUF Morgon Jean Descombes 1995 **$10** Kirsch and spice flavors are vivid in this unusually dense Beaujolais with a firm tannic underpinning.

87 GEORGES DUBOEUF Brouilly Château de Nervers 1995 **$10** Round and quite rich, showing good concentration for a Brouilly. Flavors of ripe plum and chocolate. Delicious now.

87 GEORGES DUBOEUF Brouilly Château de Pierreux Comte de Toulgoët 1995 **$10** Alluring aromas of ripe fruit, toast and spice pave the way for ripe fruit and pleasantly gamy flavors and round tannins. Big and meaty, it shows the serious side of Beaujolais.

87 GEORGES DUBOEUF Régnié Domaine du Potet 1995 **$8.50** Distinctive. Attractive floral and bell pepper aromas, ripe cherry and chocolate flavors. Thick on the palate, with solid tannins beneath. Juicy and rich.

✪ = Widest availability (over 15,000 cases produced)

86 GEORGES DUBOEUF Brouilly Flower Label 1995 **$9.50** Bright and fruity, perfumed with berry and floral aromas, this light, silky wine is perfect for summer afternoon quaffing. ✪

86 GEORGES DUBOEUF Juliénas Domaine de la Seigneurie de Juliénas 1995 **$9.50** Plush velvety texture, bright berry and floral flavors and a refreshing acidity combine to make this a soft, winning wine. Chill and enjoy.

85 GEORGES DUBOEUF Beaujolais-Villages Domaine du Granit Bleu 1995 **$8** Ripe fruit and round tannins give good texture on the palate. Plenty of plum flavors, accented with smoky, gamy notes. Crisp acidity keeps it lively. Drink now or hold.

85 GEORGES DUBOEUF Chiroubles Château de Javernand 1995 **$10** Supple yet thick-textured, with spicy bright cherry and smoky flavors. Vivid and rich, it's a bit heavy for a Chiroubles, but shows good balance nonetheless.

85 GEORGES DUBOEUF Côte-de-Brouilly Domaine de la Feuillée 1995 **$9.50** Juicy black cherry and plum flavors are bright and balanced in this typical Beaujolais. It's light enough to serve as an apéritif, but firm enough for food.

85 GEORGES DUBOEUF Juliénas Flower Label 1995 **$9** Pretty blackcherry and floral aromas carry through to the palate in this fresh, fruity red. The tannins are firm, and light banana and herbal notes emerge on the finish.

85 GEORGES DUBOEUF Morgon Flower Label 1995 **$9** A smoky note adds interest to this juicy, well-concentrated wine. The blackcherry and light herbal flavors are fresh and linger on the finish.

85 GEORGES DUBOEUF Régnié Flower Label 1995 **$8** Supple, yet shows good concentration and balance. Black cherry and smoke flavors, with firm underlying tannins. Will bloom when drunk with food.

85 LÉONARD DE ST.-AUBIN Beaujolais-Villages 1995 **$9** A bit more sophisticated than many Beaujolais-Villages. Supple, with understated cherry and citrus flavors, accented by spicy, smoky notes. Flavors bloom on the finish.

84 PAUL CINQUIN Régnié Domaine des Braves 1994 **$10** Aging well; attractive dried cherry, herb and toast flavors and still-fresh tannins. Finish is a bit dry, but this is a good food-wine.

84 GEORGES DUBOEUF Beaujolais-Villages Château de Varennes 1995 **$8** Vivid, mouthfilling flavors of plums and cherries. Clean and fresh, it's round in texture but has a firm backbone of tannin.

84 GEORGES DUBOEUF Beaujolais-Villages Château des Vierres 1995 **$8** Bright and fruity, with some depth. Ripe black cherry and grape flavors are appealing, and it has a nice balance of spice and tannin.

84 GEORGES DUBOEUF Côte-de-Brouilly Flower Label 1995 **$9** Polished and silky. Attractive floral and cherry aromas and flavors are a bit subdued right now, but show good balance.

84 PAUL JANIN Beaujolais-Villages Domaine des Vignes des Jumeaux 1994 **$10** Smoky, gamy aromas give way to flavors of plum, bitter chocolate and light earth in this tannic red. Not as fruity as a typical Beaujolais, but has good concentration. Try with grilled meats.

84 MOMMESSIN Beaujolais-Villages 1995 **$9.50** Pretty berry and spice aromas give way to fresh cherry flavors and a meaty texture, with bright acidity and firm tannins. This has punch.

83 GEORGES DUBOEUF Beaujolais-Villages Flower Label 1995 **$7.50** Straightforward and sturdy, with balance, structure and somewhat muted black cherry flavors. **○**

83 GEORGES DUBOEUF Chiroubles Flower Label 1995 **$9.50** Typical Chiroubles—light, bright and pretty. Cherry, citrus and smoky flavors suffuse the palate, then fade quickly, leaving somewhat dry tannins.

81 LOUIS JADOT Beaujolais-Villages 1995 **$10** Brawny for a Beaujolais. Meaty texture and firm tannins show promise, but the fruit flavors are obscured. A bit clumsy. **○**

Bordeaux

85 CHÂTEAU LA FONTAINE Fronsac Red 1993 **$9.00** A robust wine that combines good structure with plenty of flesh and spicy fruit. The finish is lingering. Drink now.

85 LA TERRASSE Bordeaux Supérieur La Terrasse sur la Rivière Red 1993 **$9.00** Pleasing black currant and plum flavors plus a dash of herbs and tobacco and medium body add up to a tasty wine for drinking now.

84 CHÂTEAU DE FONTENILLE Bordeaux Red 1993 **$10.00** Spice and plum aromas lead to herbal-tinged berry flavors, all wrapped up in a concentrated yet balanced presentation. Drinkable now.

83 CHÂTEAU CARSIN Premières Côtes de Bordeaux 1993 **$8.00** This vivid red offers attractive plum, floral and spicy aromas and flavors. Nicely balanced, with modest structure. Drinkable now.

83 PIERRE DOURTHE Bordeaux Numero 1 Red 1993 **$9.00** Plenty of cassis and berry character, medium to full body, silky tannins and fruity finish. A serious merchant blend for the vintage. Drinkable now.

83 CHÂTEAU HAUT REDON Bordeaux 1994 **$9.00** Bordeaux flavors and Beaujolais structure. The fresh plum and grape flavors have herbal and smoky accents.

83 CHÂTEAU HAUT-MAZIERES Bordeaux Red 1993 **$9.00** Attractive berry and spicy aromas give way to fresh fruit flavors backed by a pleasant toasty accent. It's light but balanced and firm enough for food.

83 MARQUIS DE CHASSE Bordeaux Reserve Red 1993 **$8.00** Offers toast, coffee and tobacco aromas and flavors, with firm tannins and a chewy texture. Has concentration and a lingering finish.

82 CHÂTEAU BONNET Bordeaux Réserve 1993 **$10.00** Lovely, balanced plum, black cherry and vanilla aromas and flavors, medium body, fine tannins and a fresh finish. Try now.

81 CHÂTEAU DE CARLES Fronsac 1993 **$10.00** Straightforward dried cherry and wet earth aromas and flavors, medium body, silky tannins and fresh finish. Drinkable now.

81 CHÂTEAU JONQUEYRES Bordeaux Supérieur Red 1992 **$10.00** Licorice aromas and flavors are consistent throughout this wine. Has a chewy texture, but it's still a bit simple.

81 CHÂTEAU LA GRANGEOTTE Bordeaux Red 1993 **$9.00** Bright black cherry and firm underlying tannins give this good definition and balance. Drinkable now.

80 AUGEY Bordeaux 1993 **$7.00** Sturdy and simple, with rustic tannins, but enough berry and cherry show through to make it drinkable, especially with food.

80 CHÂTEAU LA GRANGE CLINET Premières Côtes de Bordeaux 1993 **$8.00** Supple and shows off fresh berry flavors and hints of nutmeg. Has the polish of Bordeaux without much depth.

Rhône

88 DOMAINE DE L'ESPIGOUETTE Côtes du Rhône Vieilles Vignes Red 1993 **$9.00** Strong backbone of acidity and tannins. Plum and black cherry are accented by coffee and spice notes. Drinkable now.

86 DOMAINE LE COUROULU Vacqueyras Red 1992 **$10.00** Ripe plum, smoky and herbal aromas and flavors are expressive and fresh; the wine is light but graceful, with light tannins and focused fruit. Drinkable now.

85 PAUL JABOULET AÎNÉ Côtes du Ventoux Red 1993 **$7.00** Earthy and leathery, including a wallop of tannin as well. Full-bodied, rich plum and chocolate flavors; needs some time to smoothen.

84 DOMAINE ST.-LUC Coteaux du Tricastin Red 1993 **$8.00** Fruity, generous and simply delicious. This medium-bodied red goes down easily because of its light tannins and ample cherry and berry flavors.

83 DOMAINE ROUX PERE & FILS Côtes du Rhône La Berberine 1994 **$8.00** Fresh and fruity, almost like Beaujolais with its abundant berry flavors accented by black pepper. It has light tannins and should be drunk while it's fresh.

82 M. CHAPOUTIER Côtes du Rhône Belleruche 1994 **$10.00** Bright and fruity, marked by cherry, berry and cider flavors and moderate tannins. Enough depth and body to be mouth-filling. Drinkable now.

80 DOMAINE PAUL AUTARD Côtes du Rhône 1994 **$8.00** Tastes candied and bit oxidized, but has some good ripe plum and cherry fruit flavors. Lacks integration now, but could come together. Try now.

Other Red

85 CHÂTEAU HAUTERIVE LE HAUT Corbières 1993 **$10.00** Pretty black cherry flavors are spiced by cinnamon and orange peel accents in this soft, attractive red. Not big, but it has a distinctive personality. Drink now.

WHITE

Alsace

88 J.B. ADAM Riesling Alsace Réserve 1993 **$9.00** Opulent for a Riesling and at an incredible price for its quality. This round wine offers ripe, almost earthy aromas and flavors of ripe peaches and apricots wrapped around a firm core of mineral character. Drinkable now and should improve with age.

87 FRÉRES BLANCK Gewürztraminer Alsace 1994 **$10.00** Spicy and extremely perfumed with good litchi nut and baked apple flavors. Interesting and forceful, with an intense finish marked by clove and nutmeg.

87 DOMAINES SCHLUMBERGER Pinot Blanc Alsace 1993 **$10.00** Exotic accents of honey and pineapple feature this especially ripe and fruity-tasting Pinot Blanc. It's almost like Chardonnay, as its buttery notes linger on the finish. ✪

86 J.B. ADAM Sylvaner Alsace Réserve 1993 **$9.00** This has a distinctive personality, fresh fruit and mineral nuances that make it complex. Has great balance and plenty of flavor interest.

86 MEYER-FONNE Pinot Blanc Alsace 1993 **$10.00** True-to-type Pinot Blanc, dry and full-bodied, tasting like melons, almonds and minerals; adds fine tangy acidity and a lingering finish.

85 FRÉRES BLANCK Riesling Alsace 1994 **$10.00** Fresh and lively, with nice apple, mint and pineapple flavors that linger on the finish. Satisfying and delicious; it has some body as well.

85 MEYER-FONNE Sylvaner Alsace 1993 **$10.00** Fresh and lively, a full-flavored white showing apple and lemon notes accented by mineral and earth tones.

85 PIERRE SPARR Riesling Alsace Carte D'Or 1993 **$10.00** Great balance and subtle fruit make this lively and elegant. It has delicate apple aromas and rather lean, lemony flavors.

84 J.B. ADAM Muscat Alsace Réserve 1993
$10.00 Quite flavorful but unusual, offering fragrant,
floral aromas and bright notes of mint and peach that
turn slightly nutty on the finish. Very fresh and tangy.

84 J.B. ADAM Pinot Blanc Alsace Réserve 1993
$9.50 Dry and earthy, but intriguing. The funky
aroma is somewhat difficult, but apricot and peach
flavors emerge in the palate and linger on aftertaste,
blending mineral accents.

84 FRÉRES BLANCK Tokay Pinot Gris Alsace
1994 **$10.00** Fairly rich, with good melon and green
peach flavors, and a nice honeyed quality as well.
Laced with a distinctive earthiness. Not for everyone,
but still tasty.

83 LEON BEYER Pinot Blanc Alsace de Blancs
1994 **$10.00** Smooth, medium-bodied and well bal-
anced, showing earth and mineral notes and an under-
lying lemony acidity. Not showy, but flavorful in a
subtle way. ✪

Bordeaux

87 CHÂTEAU HAUT-MAZIERES Bordeaux
White 1993 **$10.00** If you like the spice that new
oak adds, you'll like this very aromatic, very high-
profile and interesting white wine. It has solid fig and
mango flavors and good balance. Drink through 1997.

86 CHÂTEAU CARSIN Bordeaux White 1994
$8.00 Classy fruit flavors and great balance make this
a very good white wine. It has fig, citrus and mango
flavors for a refreshing mix.

84 AUGEY Bordeaux White 1994 **$7.00** This has a nice, crisp balance and round texture and subtle flavors of fig, citrus and mineral that linger on the finish.

84 CHÂTEAU BONNET Entre-Deux-Mers 1994 **$8.00** Intense Sauvignon character, with grassy aromas and flavors, supported by lime accents. Medium-bodied, fresh in acidity and light on the finish.

84 CHÂTEAU DE HAUX Bordeaux White 1994 **$10.00** An unusual but appealing white Bordeaux that's bright and fragrant, with honey, vanilla and apricot flavors and plenty of richness.

84 MAITRE D'ESTOURNEL Bordeaux White 1993 **$9.00** A nice, clean, crisp white Bordeaux that has zingy grapefruit flavors and a refreshing balance.

84 MICHEL LYNCH Bordeaux White 1994 **$8.00** Lovely and elegant, with honey, strawberry, rose petal and apricot aromas and flavors. Medium body, fine acidity and a fresh finish.

83 CHÂTEAU COUCHEROY Pessac-Léognan White 1994 **$10.00** Round and creamy, offering pear, apple and lemon flavors in a medium-bodied frame offset by moderate acidity. Plenty of pear in the aftertaste.

80 CHÂTEAU DE CHARRON Bordeaux White 1994 **$8.00** An unassuming white with subtle fig and citrus flavors and a short finish. Clean and simple.

Burgundy

87 CHARTRON & TRÉBUCHET Bourgogne Chardonnay 1994 **$10.00** Wonderful for a simple Bourgogne. Fresher than many '94s, sporting juicy, succulent, mouthpuckering flavors of lime, pear and ripe apple and a long finish. Drinkable now through 1998.

84 GEORGES BURRIER Chardonnay Mâcon-Villages 1994 **$10.00** Rich and honeyed with plenty of spice and ripe apple flavors. Lacks intensity and depth, but has some nice fennel and licorice notes.

81 JEAN CLAUDE BOISSET Chardonnay de Bourgogne; Charles de France White 1993 **$10.00** A bit lean and green, yet showing pleasant mineral, chalk, pear and fig notes. It delivers good flavor intensity, but seems somewhat muted on the finish.

80 JEAN CLAUDE BOISSET Mâcon-Blanc-Villages White 1994 **$8.00** Lavishly oaked, standing out with its full, ripe, sweet-tasting vanilla and toast notes. The wood may get tiring; slightly astringent finish.

Loire: Muscadet

86 SAUVION & FILS Muscadet de Sèvre et Maine Sur Lie Sauvion du Cléray 1995 **$7.00** A ripe, exotic style, that delivers loads of peach and grilled almond aromas and flavors. Not typical perhaps, yet it makes a very intriguing value nonetheless. ✪

85 LES FRERES COUILLAUD Muscadet de Sèvre et Maine Sur Lie Château La Morinière 1994 **$10.00** Surprising depth and freshness, delivering almond and green apple flavors that segue into a firm, slightly bitter finish. Well made.

85 SAUVION & FILS Muscadet de Sèvre et Maine Sur Lie Château du Cléray 1995 **$9.00** Fresh and crisp, showing a hint of creaminess on the palate. Melon and herb flavors linger on the finish. Just what to look for in a Muscadet.

84 LOUIS METAIREAU Muscadet de Sèvre et Maine Sur Lie Carte Noire 1990 **$10.00** Mature character adds complexity, offering nuances of butterscotch, citrus and herb, but the finish is tart. Not for everyone.

84 SAUVION & FILS Muscadet de Sèvre et Maine Sur Lie Carte d'Or 1995 **$7.00** The melon and marzipan flavors are balanced by moderate acidity, keeping this white fresh and lively. Enjoyable now. ✪

83 CHÂTEAU DE LA DIMERIE Muscadet de Sèvre et Maine 1994 **$7.00** There'a a note of maturity here that brings out herbal and petrol elements. Still, it's balanced and lively. Drink up.

83 LES FRERES COUILLAUD Muscadet de Sèvre et Maine Sur Lie Domaine La Morinière 1994 **$9.00** Developed flavors of pine and herb are matched by a firm structure. Drink this with oysters or light seafood.

Loire: Vouvray

83 BARTON & GUESTIER Vouvray 1993
$10.00 This lively wine has a nice mix of honeyed
sweetness and crisp acidity, with peach and mineral
accents. It's not rich, but lingers on the finish.

83 NICOLAS Vouvray White 1993 **$6.00**
Attractive aromas of wildflower honey give way to a
smooth texture on the palate, with honey, melon and
light citrus flavors. It has some richness and just a
touch of sweetness.

82 ROBERT MICHELE Vouvray Les Trois Fils
White 1993 **$7.00** There are pretty floral and peachy
flavors here, enlivened by lemony acidity, but an
earthy note detracts. It's got good weight on the
palate, and finishes dry.

Loire: Other

85 LES FRERES COUILLAUD Chardonnay Vin
de Pays du Jardin de la France Domaine La
Morinière 1995 **$8.50** Broad aromas and flavors of
ripe apple, peach and butter are the hallmarks of this
soft, easy-drinking white. There's good complexity
and a moderate finish.

82 LES FRERES COUILLAUD Vin de Pays du
Jardin de la France Chardet 1995 **$9.00** A nutty,
creamy, buttery note dominates, detracting from the
freshness, but there's depth and balance. Good as a
summertime quaff.

80 LES FRERES COUILLAUD Chardonnay Vin de Pays du Jardin de la France Domaine Trois Frères 1994 **$8.00** Very ripe honey and lanolin flavors. It's rich, yet the finish is just a touch bitter.

Other White

82 DOMAINE MAX AUBERT Côtes du Rhône Domaine de la Présidente Blanc de Blancs 1994 **$10.00** A substantial dry white Rhône offering subtle floral, figgy aromas and flavors, smooth, rich texture but only modest notes.

82 LA BOUVERIE Costières de Nimes White 1994 **$6.00** Pleasant and fruity, showing some nice buttery notes and almond and peach flavors that linger through the finish.

82 CHÂTEAU PLANERES Côtes du Roussillon White 1994 **$8.00** Richly-textured and rustic, but it's appealing, with flavors of pears, almonds and herbs that linger on the finish.

80 ARMAND ROUX Picpoul de Pinet Coteaux du Languedoc 1994 **$7.00** An assertive wine that offers flavors of almonds, smoke and figs and a tart, acidic core. It has personality without refinement. ✪

Blush

85 GEORGES DUBOEUF Vin de Pays d'Oc Syrah 1994 **$6.00** Banana and watermelon are the predominant aromas, and the flavors are surprisingly concentrated—full of spicy raspberry and cherry. Finishes dry.

85 CHÂTEAU VAL JOANIS Côtes du Lubéron Rosé 1993 **$8.00** A bright, fruity, berry character and a touch of spice offset the firm, dry texture. It is balanced for matching with light summer food. ✪

80 FORTANT DE FRANCE Vin de Pays d'Oc Rosé Syrah 1994 **$7.00** Dry and earthy, its flavors dominated by dried cherry and spice. Seems very full-bodied.

Sparkling

86 VARICHON & CLERC Blanc de Blancs 1992 **$10.00** Lively texture and nicely fruity character at reasonable rates. This well-balanced French sparkling wine reminds us a lot of Chardonnay. It has fresh apple and pear flavors accented by vanilla, leading into a lingering finish.

81 CHARLES DE FÈRE Brut Chardonnay Tradition NV **$10.00** A refreshing bottle of bubbly with crisp, lean apple and lemon flavors and a lively feel from effervescence and generous acidity.

80 HENRI DE GRAMEY Brut Saumur NV
$10.00 Clean and simple, offering modest fig, honey
and apple notes. A bit soft, but flavorful and easy to
drink. ✪

RED WINES BY GRAPE VARIETY

Cabernet Sauvignon

85 JEAN CLAUDE BOISSET Cabernet
Sauvignon Vin de Pays d'Oc 1994 **$6.00** The
blackberry and chocolate flavors are ripe and appealing in this lush French wine, and the round tannins
give support without astringency. The bargain price
also adds to the appeal. Drinkable now.

84 F. CHAUVENET Cabernet Sauvignon Vin de
Pays d'Oc 1994 **$9.00** Polished and ripe, offering
cassis and light tobacco notes and enough structure
for food in a pretty, well-integrated package. Good for
drinking now.

84 CHEVALIER DE RODILAN Vin de Pays d'Oc
1994 **$6.00** This French red is loaded with tannins
that are layered through its blackberry and plum flavors. It has an elegant aroma, with a spicy finish.
Drink now.

84 LES JAMELLES Cabernet Sauvignon Vin de
Pays d'Oc 1994 **$7.00** Solid black cherry, tobacco
and black olive notes and firm tannins. Rich, sturdy,
well integrated if not complex.

83 BARON PHILIPPE DE ROTHSCHILD
Cabernet Sauvignon Vin de Pays d'Oc 1994
$10.00 Dominated by herbal aromas and flavors.
Medium-bodied and fairly well balanced, finishing
with a hint of chocolate and spice.

82 MOMMESSIN Cabernet Sauvignon Vin de
Pays d'Oc 1993 **$6.50** Black cherry, herbal and
smoky aromas lead to a light, smooth, well-integrated
palate. This doesn't show much fruit, but it's balanced
and drinking well now.

80 BARTON & GUESTIER Cabernet Sauvignon
Vin de Pays d'Oc 1994 **$6.00** Smooth raisin, spice
and tobacco flavors. Seems very advanced for a 1994,
but it's harmonious and the spice notes linger on aftertaste.

80 ALEXIS LICHINE Cabernet Sauvignon Vin
de Pays d'Oc 1993 **$6.00** An herbal-scented, plum-
flavored, tough-textured red that is simple and sturdy.
Drinkable now.

Merlot

84 LA BOUVERIE Merlot Vin de Pays d'Oc
Cuvée Spéciale 1993 **$7.00** Well made and well
priced, this French red offers balanced black cherry,
herb and spice flavors, firm but not overbearing tannins and a lingering, smoky finish. Drinkable now.

84 GEORGES DUBOEUF Merlot Domaine de Bordeneuve Vin de Pays d'Oc 1994 **$7.00** Dark and tannic, with attractive aromas and flavors of smoke, cherry and herbs. Has enough complexity of flavor, but firm with tannins. Try now.

84 NICOLAS Maison Nicolas Réserve Merlot Vin de Pays d'Oc 1993 **$6.00** The plum and chocolate flavors have good concentration in this fresh-tasting French Merlot, and the tannins have mellowed, which allows the fruit to linger on the finish. A harmonious wine that doesn't break the bank. ✪

83 CHEVALIER DE RODILAN Merlot Vin de Pays d'Oc 1994 **$6.00** A good effort. Rich, vibrant and fresh with plenty of plum and berry flavors. Has good concentration, but a little short on the finish.

83 DELAS Merlot Vin de Pays d'Oc 1993 **$9.00** Smooth drinking and nicely flavored, with blackberry and cherry accents and light tannins. Rich fruit, appealing texture, and drinkable now.

83 GEORGES DUBOEUF Merlot Vin de Pays d'Oc 1994 **$7.00** Deep in color, smoky and herbal in aroma, with modest plum and licorice flavors and moderate tannins. Enjoyable and drinkable now.

83 FORTANT DE FRANCE Merlot Vin de Pays d'Oc 1994 **$7.00** Appealing blackberry and smoke aromas carry through on the soft, full palate, though lean tannins on the finish detract. Ripe and flavorful.

83 MOMMESSIN Merlot Vin de Pays d'Oc 1993 **$6.50** Soft, round, typical black cherry and light herbal flavors, reminiscent of a Bordeaux petit château in character. It's drinking well now. ✪

82 BARTON & GUESTIER Merlot Vin de Pays d'Oc 1994 **$6.00** Solid and straightforward, featuring cherry, herb and chocolate flavors and enough tannin for grip. Not complex, but a modest complement for grilled meats.

82 LES JAMELLES Merlot Vin de Pays d'Oc 1994 **$7.00** Ripe, fleshy, sporting jammy prune and chocolate flavors and firm tannins on aftertaste. Sacrifices elegance for power, but comes up a bit short on the finish. ✪

82 BARON PHILIPPE DE ROTHSCHILD Merlot Vin de Pays d'Oc 1994 **$10.00** A workmanlike wine with modest chocolate, cherry and plum flavors. Well balanced and still a bit tannic. It finishes on an astringent note.

81 RICHEMONT Merlot Vin de Pays d'Oc 1993 **$6.00** Black olive and herbal flavors give this a distinctive personality. Fleshy and firmly tannic, but needing more fruit for balance and winding up somewhat clumsy. Try now.

81 SALLE DE COEURS Merlot Vin de Pays d'Oc 1994 **$8.00** Ripe plum, meat and tomato flavors offer roundness without much stuffing, and a lean streak of tannin dominates the finish. Best accompanying food.

Syrah

84 LES JAMELLES Syrah Vin de Pays d'Oc 1994 **$7.00** Ripe, almost jammy, this offers pleasant blackberry, licorice and tar flavors and round, lush tannins, adding an attractive smoky finish. Drinkable now.

83 RICHEMONT Syrah Vin de Pays d'Oc 1993 **$6.00** There's plenty of ripe blackberry flavor here, soft and almost sweet on the palate. It resembles an Australian Shiraz, without the weight. Drink now.

80 JEAN CLAUDE BOISSET Syrah Vin de Pays d'Oc 1994 **$6.00** Licorice and gamy aromas say Syrah, and while the flavors are a bit lean and tannins somewhat dry, this is true to the variety. Straightforward and drinkable now.

Other Red

80 PAYSAGE Galet Vineyards Red Vin de Pays d'Oc 1993 **$10.00** Light, simple cherry flavor and soft tannins. It's balanced and adds a pleasant, spicy finish. Drink now.

White Wines by Grape Variety

Chardonnay and Chardonnay Blend

86 F. CHAUVENET Chardonnay Vin de Pays d'Oc 1994 **$8.00** Though not flamboyant, this solid white is clean and vibrant with ripe fruit. Vanilla and hazelnut flavors mingle with melon and floral notes, and the citrusy acidity keeps it fresh. Good value in a French white.

86 GEORGES DUBOEUF Chardonnay Vin de Pays d'Oc 1994 **$7.00** A touch of oak adds interest, and toasty flavors that complement the apple flavor. It's clean and well-balanced. A classy wine for the appellation. Slight bottle variation noted.

85 RICHEMONT Chardonnay Vin de Pays d'Oc 1994 **$6.00** Exuberant aromas of tropical fruit and vanilla give this French white an almost Australian character, which follows through on the round, nearly sweet palate. It's not sophisticated, but a good example of a popular style at a good price. ✪

84 BARON PHILIPPE DE ROTHSCHILD Chardonnay Vin de Pays d'Oc 1994 **$10.00** Floral and vanilla aromas give way to lemon custard flavors in this smooth, balanced white. Tropical fruit accents add interest, but it finishes short.

84 FORTANT DE FRANCE Chardonnay Vin de Pays d'Oc 1994 **$8.00** A ripe, generous wine with melon and honey flavors and just enough acidity to keep it taut. Spicy, nutmeg notes add interest.

84 MOMMESSIN Chardonnay Vin de Pays d'Oc 1994 **$6.50** Crisp apple and light vanilla flavors keep this on the straight and narrow. Not much complexity, but will make a discreet partner with food. ✪

83 DOMAINE PIERRE JACQUES Chardonnay Vin de Pays d'Oc 1993 **$8.00** There are toasty and nutty accents to the pear and mineral flavors in this firm, smooth wine. Still lively, though a bit short.

83 NICOLAS Chardonnay Vin de Pays d'Oc Maison Nicolas Réserve 1994 **$6.00** This smooth wine has a nice lanolin mouth-feel that makes it generous and creamy; the attractive melon and lightly spicy flavors just could use more crispness. ✪

82 BARTON & GUESTIER Chardonnay Vin de Pays d'Oc 1994 **$9.00** Smooth and creamy, plump with vanilla, coconut and melon flavors. It lacks crispness, though.

82 KLUG Chardonnay Vin de Pays d'Oc Sélection des Grands Chais 1994 **$7.00** A lively, well-rounded white with fresh acidity and ripe melon and peach flavors. It's soft and clean.

81 CHAIS BAUMIERE Chardonnay Vin de Pays d'Oc 1994 **$6.00** This resembles an international-style Chardonnay, with vanilla, sweet melon and light apple flavors. Easy to quaff.

81 KLUG Chardonnay-Sauvignon Blanc Vin de Pays d'Oc Sélection des Grands Chais 1994 **$7.00** Combines ample fruit flavors and a fairly rich texture for a solid, straightforward character.

81 VAL D'ORBIEU Chardonnay Vin de Pays d'Oc Réserve St. Martin 1994 **$8.00** Ripe, fruity and simple, offering vanilla and melon flavors in a soft, round, straightforward style with earthy accents. **۞**

80 LES JAMELLES Chardonnay Vin de Pays d'Oc 1994 **$7.00** Vanilla and pineapple aromas are promising, but on the palate, this shuts down. Firm, smooth texture but little fruit, with a slightly bitter finish.

Sauvignon Blanc

82 RICHEMONT Sauvignon Blanc Vin de Pays d'Oc 1994 **$6.00** Soft and round in texture, with ripe, clean fruit flavor that reminds us of Chardonnay.

82 BARON PHILIPPE DE ROTHSCHILD Sauvignon Blanc Vin de Pays d'Oc 1994 **$10.00** Nicely balanced and smooth, with modest fruit flavors and nice, fresh acidity. Appealing for its crispness.

81 CHAIS BAUMIERE Sauvignon Blanc Vin de Pays d'Oc 1994 **$6.00** A ripe-tasting, clean and fresh white with ample melon and citrus flavors. Soft and easy to drink.

81 GEORGES DUBOEUF Sauvignon Vin de Pays d'Oc 1994 **$6.00** Basically neutral in flavor, but rugged and has enough body and acidity to hold its own with food. Simple and straightforward—a good refresher.

Other White

83 VAL D'ORBIEU Marsanne Vin de Pays d'Oc Réserve St. Martin 1994 **$7.00** Marsanne makes great whites in Hermitage; here it's round and generous, with floral and melon flavors. Not profound, but it brings you back for another sip. ✪

81 LA BOUVERIE Viognier Vin de Pays d'Oc Cuvée Spéciale 1993 **$8.00** A core of steely acidity gives this a refreshing intensity, along with clean, muted fruit flavors; it doesn't taste much like Viognier, though.

80 GEORGES DUBOEUF Chasan Vin de Pays d'Oc 1994 **$6.00** The floral aromas and soft peach flavors are pleasant in this soft, simple white. Shows some delicacy and would make a good apéritif.

Germany

BY BRUCE SANDERSON

Germany produces a compelling variety of
wines in 13 wine-growing regions (including two in
the former East German Republic). Selecting a
German wine appears to be a daunting task, due to
the large number of types and styles, and confusion
resulting from label nomenclature. With the help of a
few basic guidelines, however, selecting a German
wine is not difficult, given the generally high quality
standards of most producers.

Undoubtedly, the best German wines are made
from Riesling. While few of these fall into the
"under $10" category, there are still good-value
Rieslings to be found. While some originate from a
single vineyard site, such as Piesporter Goldtröpfchen,
most are usually blends of different sites, bottled
under a *Grosslagen* or collective name, for example
Zeller Schwarze Katz or Bernkasteler Kurfürstlay.
Others may be blends of two or more grape varieties.
German wine law requires a varietally labelled wine
to contain at least 85% of the specified grape variety.
Varieties commonly blended with Riesling are
Sylvaner, Müller-Thurgau and Elbling.

Müller-Thurgau is the most widely planted white
variety, and is capable of producing good value
wines if the yields are low enough to coax some
character out of the grapes. There is some red wine

production, mainly from Pinot Noir (called Spät-
burgunder in Germany), but the values are more
likely to be from varieties such as Blauer Portugieser, Trollinger and Lemberger.

WITH THE HELP OF A FEW BASIC GUIDELINES, SELECTING A GERMAN WINE IS NOT DIFFICULT.

With German wines, the region often provides an indication of style. Mosel wines tend to be the most deli-cate, Rheinhessen rounder and fruity, while Nahe wines fall somewhwere between the two. Rheingau produces firm, spicy wines.

The richest, fullest versions come from Pfalz. Because
of their vibrant acidity, fruitiness and hint of sweetness, German white wines are terrific with food, par-
ticulary seafood, chicken, pork, smoked meats and
fish, and spicy Asian dishes.

Bruce Sanderson is Wine Spectator's *tasting director.*

How to Read a German Wine Label

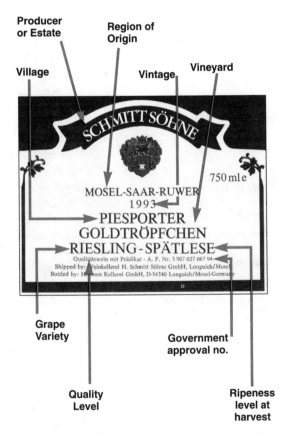

Producer or Estate

Region of Origin

Village

Vintage

Vineyard

SCHMITT SÖHNE

750 ml e

MOSEL-SAAR-RUWER
1993
PIESPORTER
GOLDTRÖPFCHEN
RIESLING - SPÄTLESE

Qualitätswein mit Prädikat - A. P. Nr. 3 907 027 067 94
Shipped by: Weinkellerei H. Schmitt Söhne GmbH, Longuich/Mosel
Bottled by: Hermen Kellerei GmbH, D-54340 Longuich/Mosel-Germany

Grape Variety

Government approval no.

Quality Level

Ripeness level at harvest

1. Mosel-Saar-Ruwer   **4.** Rheinhessen

2. Nahe   **5.** Pfalz

3. Rheingau

White

Riesling

84 CARL GRAFF Riesling Kabinett Mosel-Saar-Ruwer 1994 **$6.50** Light, almost delicate and slightly sweet, with crisp apple, peach and floral aromas and flavors. Just what you want in a kabinett.

84 CARL GRAFF Spätlese Mosel-Saar-Ruwer Erdener Treppchen 1994 **$9.00** Nicely balanced and fruity, with a pleasant sweetness and firm texture.

82 SICHEL Riesling Rheingau Bereich Johannisberg 1993 **$8.00** This is smoky and earthy in aroma, amply fruity and sweet in flavor and rather soft in texture.

81 GRAFF QbA Mosel-Saar-Ruwer Ürziger Schwarzlay 1994 **$5.00** Fresh, fruity, nearly dry, with smoky citrus aromas, straightforward fruit flavors and a lively texture.

80 SICHEL Riesling Pfalz 1993 **$8.00** This Riesling is austere, with herbal, smoky aromas and crisp grapefruit flavors. Off-dry.

80 SICHEL Riesling White Pfalz 1993 **$6.00** Evolved aromas of petrol and pine show some maturity in this dry Riesling. There's good typicity, but lacks the fruit to balance the earth and petrol flavors.

✪ = Widest availability (over 15,000 cases produced)

Other White

86 VALCKENBERG Madonna Bereich Wonnegau Rheinhessen 1994 **$7.50** An attractive white blend from Germany that offers generous aromas of apricot and pineapple, lots of fruit flavor and lingering hints of honey and apricot on the finish. Nicely balanced with fresh acidity, at an agreeable price.

83 VALCKENBERG Pinot Blanc Rheinhessen 1994 **$6.00** A tart, bracing, dry Pinot Blanc with vivid grapefruit flavor and firm acidity. Smells ripe and exotic, turns leaner on the palate, but has depth.

82 SICHEL Pinot Gris Pfalz 1993 **$8.00** A distinctive, very dry white with an intriguing, doughy aroma, unusual mineral flavors and a bitter-almond finish.

81 BLUE NUN Liebfraumilch Pfalz 1993 **$6.00** A soft and fruity white with plenty of citrus and peach flavors and some honey on the finish. Easy to drink.

81 SICHEL Mosel-Saar-Ruwer Zeller Schwarze Katz 1993 **$8.00** Light and pleasant, with peachy, smoky aromas and similar flavors. A touch of honey on the finish.

80 PRINZ ZU SALM-DALBERG QbA Nahe 1994 **$7.50** Clean, fresh and lively, with herbal and citrus flavors, a hint of sweetness, medium body and soft texture.

Italy

By Per-Henrik Mansson

More than any other European country, Italy has come of age in recent years as a producer of high quality—and sometimes very expensive—wines. Yet riding on the coattails of the more famous wines are a slew of great values. Italy already has a favorable climate and fine vineyard land. Now, improvements to wine cellars and vineyards have enabled the Italians to compete in the world marketplace.

From Piedmont in the north to Sicily in the south, Italy is a cornucopia of wine regions that grow dozens of indigenous grape varieties. To be sure, Cabernet Sauvignon, Chardonnay and Merlot are making some inroads, but these are a drop in the bucket compared to wines made with local varieties.

Italian wine labels often fail to mention the grapes used to make the wine. For example, the backbone of Chianti Classico is Sangiovese, a grape that produces a red wine with a refreshing, crisp texture. But several other grape varieties are included as well, and the percentages can change from year to year.

The geographic origins of Italian wines are prominently highlighted on the labels. Thus, names such as Barolo, Chianti Classico and Brunello di Montalcino indicate the regulated districts, or appellations, that the wines come from.

The Piedmont region, with its upscale Barolo and Barbaresco, and Tuscany, with its Brunello di

Montalcino, produce the bulk of the expensive red Italian wines exported to the United States. Yet these regions also produce their fair share of good values.

While the Chianti district in Tuscany used to be known for its great values, today most of the better Chiantis cost more than $10. Instead, you can look for varietal wines labeled Sangiovese that are grown outside of Chianti. This grape variety is the mainstay of Chianti, so the taste is usually similar.

When the price is right, we have a weakness for Dolcetto and Barbera, two Piedmont grape varieties that produce deliciously grapey, very aromatic and not-too-tannic wines. A dozen producers make fine Dolcettos and Barberas at attractive prices in top years; among them is Pio Cesare.

Valpolicella, a wine region just outside Verona in northeastern Italy, makes a juicy, soft red primarily from the Corvina grape. Even better is the Valpolicella Classico. The best of these, like a good vintage from producer Bertani, will retail for under $10 and score very well in *Wine Spectator* tastings.

Although the real action in Italy is in red wines, the white wines of northeastern Italy are making progress, as evidenced by the Pinot Grigios from Peter Zemmer and Pagio.

Like no other cuisine in the world, Italian cooking lends itself to light, youthful and often inexpensive wine. What better match for pasta, risotto or pizza than a glass of fresh, vibrant, slightly chilled Chianti Classico, Dolcetto, Barbera, Valpolicella or Rosso di Montalcino? Or try a thirst-quenching white like Soave, Pinot Grigio or Verdicchio with grilled fish sprinkled lightly with olive oil and lemon juice.

Per-Henrik Mansson is a senior editor of Wine Spectator.

Most Reliable Values

These wines have proven to be of consistently good quality, year in and year out. Even if a particular vintage is not reviewed here, you may purchase these wines with confidence.

RED WINES

Cappezzana Chianti Montalbano

Capezzana Conti Contini Sangiovese di Toscana

Casal Thaulero Montepulciano d'Abruzzo

Castello Banfi Rosso di Montalcino Centine

Castello Di Querceto Chianti Classico

Castello Di Volpaia Chianti Borgianni

Dr. Cosimo Taurino Riserva Salice Salentino Red

WHITE WINES

Anselmi Soave Classico Superiore San Vincenzo

Antinori Castello della Sala Chardonnay

Bollini Grave del Friuli Reserve Selection Pinot
   Grigio

Casa Girelli Trentino I Mesi Chardonnay

Cinzano Asti Spumante NV

Tosti Asti Spumante NV

How to Read an Italian Wine Label

Brand or Proprietary Name

Grape Variety

Region of Origin

Producer or Estate

Vintage

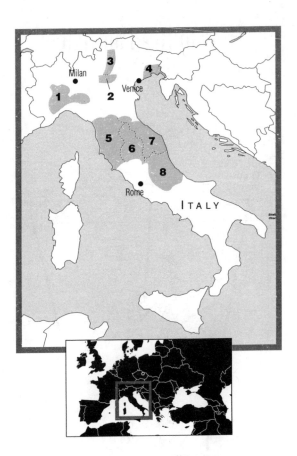

1. Piedmont (Piemonte):
   Barbera, Dolcetto

2. Verona: Bardolino,
   Soave, Valpolicella

3. Trentino/Alto Adige

4. Friuli-Venezia

5. Tuscany: Chianti,
   Rosso di Montalcino

6. Umbria: Orvieto

7. The Marches:
   Verdicchio

8. Abruzzi:
   Montepulciano
   d'Abruzzo

RED

Cabernet Sauvignon

83 LA MARCA Cabernet Sauvignon Piave 1993 **$6.00** Hearty, super ripe flavors of prune and blackberry make this a robust wine to enjoy now while it's fresh. Fairly light in tannins, but full-bodied. ✪

82 BORGO MAGREDO Cabernet Sauvignon Grave del Friuli 1994 **$8.00** Modest cherry and bell pepper flavors dominate. Juicy and flavorful, with a note of black pepper on the finish.

82 COLLAVINI Cabernet Grave del Friuli Roncaccio 1993 **$9.00** Tastes ripe and full-bodied, with lots of cherry and berry flavor and not too much tannin. Enjoy now.

Chianti

84 CAPEZZANA Chianti Montalbano 1993 **$8.00** Firmly structured, with lots of strawberry and cherry flavors. Finishes a little earthy, but still appealing.

84 FATTORIA LE BOCCE Chianti Classico 1993 **$9.00** Fresh and delicious '93 Chianti with red berry, dried cherry and a hint of tobacco. Medium-bodied with light tannins and crisp finish. Drinkable now.

82 CARPINETO Chianti Classico 1993 **$10.00** Obviously oaky, with a big vanilla component and spiciness. A good quaff, but hard to believe it's Chianti. Modest cherry and plum flavors. Drink now. ✪

✪ = Widest availability (over 15,000 cases produced)

82 CASTELLO DI QUERCETO Chianti Classico 1992 **$9.00** Straightforward, with modest cherry and berry flavors that give way to a slightly astringent finish. A solid backbone of tannins. Drink now.

82 SPALLETTI Chianti 1993 **$7.50** Firm and flavorful, with good cherry and almond flavors. Straightforward and fairly light, though with a stemmy quality in the aroma. Drink now.

81 CASTELLO DI VOLPAIA Chianti Borgianni 1992 **$8.00** Full-bodied, with cherry and plum flavors. Simple and cleanly made, but nothing to get excited about.

Dolcetto d'Alba/Barbera d'Alba

86 RENATO RATTI Dolcetto d'Alba 1993 **$10.00** Ripe and round; marries its lush blackberry flavors with a light earthiness. Good balance of fruit and tannin, and impressive concentration. Drink now.

83 CA' DE MONTE Dolcetto d'Alba 1993 **$8.00** Cherry and nutmeg flavors brightened by lively acidity. A brisk and light-bodied red that's fresh and ready to drink.

83 PIO CESARE Dolcetto d'Alba Red 1992 **$10.00** Attractive plum and floral aromas, with some depth to the plum and cherry flavors, but it finishes a bit hollow and dry. Still pleasurable, though.

83 FONTANAFREDDA Barbera d'Alba Red 1990 **$10.00** Interesting mature aromas of truffles and mushrooms. Flavors of dried cherries turn a bit astringent on the finish. Almost over the hill. ✪

82 TENUTE COLUE Barbera d'Alba Red 1992 **$10.00** A very rustic style, with dried cherry and stewed plum flavors. A little dull and a bit astringent, but quaint.

Merlot

83 FONTANA CANDIDA Merlot della Tre Venezie 1994 **$8.00** A polished wine that has a nice mix of smoky, herbal flavors of black cherry and shows balance between its bright acidity and light tannins. Drinkable now.

82 BOLLA Merlot Piave 1994 **$8.00** Light and fresh, showing pretty berry and cherry flavors along with bright acidity and light tannins. It's fruity and refreshing; drinkable now.

81 CANTINE MEZZACORONA Merlot Trentino 1993 **$8.00** A rich but rustic style of wine with earthy, spicy flavors, firm tannins and a short finish.

81 TORRESELLA Merlot 1993 **$9.00** Earthy and herbaceous flavors dominate in this lean, firm red. Not showing much fruit now, but has some concentration; try in late 1996.

80 LA MARCA Novello Merlot del Veneto Piave Red 1995 **$6.00** Raspberry and tutti-fruity flavors dominate this fresh wine. Light in tannins.

Montepulciano d'Abruzzo

88 ANTONIO & ELIO MONTI Montepulciano d'Abruzzo 1993 **$10.00** What a treat. An amazingly deep and intense wine for this region. It's packed with blackberry, herb, spice and smoke flavors, tannic but still smooth in texture. Drink through 1998.

87 SANTANGELO Colli del Moro Montepulciano d'Abruzzo 1992 **$10.00** A broad, amply flavored red that's generous, spicy, tannic but smooth enough to drink now while the cherry, blackberry and floral flavors stay fresh.

85 FARNESE Montepulciano d'Abruzzo 1993 **$5.00** Smooth, spicy, almost plush in texture, with good cherry flavors and nice balance. An Italian red that is easy to enjoy now. ✪

85 MASCIARELLI Montepulciano d'Abruzzo 1993 **$6.00** Fresh, lively and packed with fruit flavor. A bargain red from Italy that shows deep color, lots of cherry and berry notes, firm acidity and moderate tannins. ✪

84 VILLA FIORE Montepulciano d'Abruzzo 1993 **$4.50** An intensely fruity red with vibrant cherry and anise flavors, moderate tannins and a smooth texture. Fine to drink now.

82 CASAL THAULERO Montepulciano d'Abruzzo 1993 **$6.00** A robust, hearty red with lots of cherry flavor, crisp acidity and firm tannins. Drink now while it's fresh. ✪

81 SCARLATTA Montepulciano d'Abruzzo 1993 **$4.00** A hearty but simple red with moderate tannins, modest raspberry flavors and medium body.

Sangiovese

86 CAPEZZANA Conti Contini Sangiovese di Toscana 1993 **$9.00** A flavorful cherry and plum palate is layered with tobacco and spice. Fresh and lively, with well-integrated tannins. Plenty of stuffing here; drink now.

84 ROMANDIOLA Il Pavone D'Oro Superiore Sangiovese di Romagna 1993 **$7.50** A good, full-bodied wine with modest tannins. It is fruity and has some nice plum flavors and a touch of brown sugar. Mature and ready to drink.

83 UMBERTO CESARI Riserva Sangiovese di Romagna 1992 **$10.00** Firm and moderately tannic, with an nice core of cherry flavors. Simple, but solid. ✪

82 BOLLA Sangiovese di Romagna 1994 **$6.00** Simple and fruity, with some nice raspberry and pepper flavors. Fresh, with a good, clean finish. ✪

82 CECCHI Sangiovese di Toscana 1993 **$6.00** Firm structure, with cranberry and currant flavors. Fairly rich, concentrated and tart on the finish. ✪

Valpolicella

87 BERTANI Valpantena Valpolicella Secco
1992 **$10.00** This is powerful for a Valpolicella, yet
retains the smoky, cherry flavors typical of the appellation. The tannins are softening, yet still firm; try it
with grilled meats. ✪

86 SANTI Solane Valpolicella Classico 1993
$8.00 Toast and vanilla flavors suggest oak aging,
which is unusual for the region, but the plum and
cherry flavors are ripe enough for balance. It shows
some tannic structure and a pleasant, spicy finish.

85 CORTE SANT'ALDA Superiore Valpolicella
1993 **$10.00** Made in a beefier style than traditional
Valpolicella, this has ripe blackberry and tar flavors
and round, firm tannins. It's fruity and still fresh.

85 GUERRIERI-RIZZARDI Valpolicella Classico
Superiore Villa Rizzardi Poiega 1993 **$7.00**
Fragrant with cherry and smoky aromas, this light,
crisp wine is balanced and still fresh, with just enough
tannin to hold up to food. Well made and typical.

85 LUIGI RIGHETTI Valpolicella Classico
Superiore Campolieti 1993 **$10.00** Ripe and
unusually concentrated for Valpolicella, with plum,
licorice, coffee and toast aromas and flavors. The tannins are a bit light for the rich flavors, but it's still
appealing. ✪

80 SANTA SOFIA Superiore Valpolicella Classico 1992 **$8.00** Very light and silky, approaching a rosé in color and structure, with strawberry and tea flavors that perk up the palate, then slip away. Try it lightly chilled.

Other Reds

89 MONTE ANTICO 1991 **$9.00** A distinctive, deeply flavorful red that shows cranberry and dried cherry character, with tight acidity and very firm tannins. Hints of spice and oak develop as you sip. Should open up with time. ✪

85 BADIA A COLTIBUONO Cancelli 1993 **$8.50** Has the whole palette of Tuscan flavors-spice, cherry, olive, herb-in an elegant package of acidity and firm tannins. It's lean and mature, so drink soon.

84 CAPEZZANA Barco Reale 1993 **$10.00** An herbal note runs through this and the dominant flavors are cranberry and green cherry. Fairly tight and still tannic; needs smoothing out. Drink now.

83 CASTELLO BANFI Rosso di Montalcino Centine 1993 **$8.00** Medium-bodied Rosso, both crisp and generous, featuring ripe, sweet-tasting plum, black cherry and lemon rind flavors that end on a medium to long finish. ✪

83 FOSSI Vanti Red 1992 **$8.00** A little light, but still flavorful, showing cherry and leather notes. Simple, pleasant and reveals modest spice notes on the finish.

82 DR. COSIMO TAURINO Riserva Salice Salentino Red 1990 **$9.00** Begins with smoky barbecue aromas, followed by a fleshy, mouth-coating texture. The flavors lean toward stewed tomato and mineral. Drinkable now.

82 TERRALE Rosso 1994 **$4.50** Attractive, straightforward and has sweet plum and cherry flavors backed by vibrant acidity. Immediately appealing. ✪

80 CASA DI PESCATORI 1993 **$5.00** A touch rustic in its simple cherry, herb and brown sugar notes, followed by a slightly tannic finish.

WHITE

Chardonnay

86 ANTINORI Chardonnay Castello della Sala 1994 **$8.00** Bright, fresh and peachlike in flavor, nicely accented by toasty oak, with good depth and a lingering aftertaste. Crisp acidity makes it especially refreshing.

85 CASA GIRELLI Chardonnay Trentino i Mesi 1994 **$9.00** Perfumed vanilla and floral aromas give way to firm flavors of melon, herb and toast in this delicate yet assertive white. Not showy, but makes you want another sip.

84 FONTANA CANDIDA Chardonnay White 1994 **$8.00** A clean, charming, smooth-textured Chardonnay that shows appealing apple and nutmeg flavors and great balance.

83 FRANZ HAAS Chardonnay Alto Adige 1993 **$10.00** Smoky and earthy in style, this crisp, austere wine makes no concessions to sweetness or even fruitiness yet manages to remain balanced and is a fine match for food.

83 MALPAGA Chardonnay Trentino 1994 **$10.00** A slightly sweet fruitiness gives this round wine immediate appeal. It's soft, with notes of peach, melon and vanilla, but it lacks the acidity for the long run. Enjoy now as an apéritif.

83 CANALETTO Chardonnay 1994 **$6.50** A pretty wine, this shows floral and almond aromas and flavors with a silky, polished texture. It's a bit soft and perfumy for food, but makes an appealing apéritif.

82 BORGO MAGREDO Chardonnay Grave del Friuli 1994 **$8.00** Fruity, floral and slightly buttery. A fresh, mouth-filling Chardonnay that's clean and refreshing.

Pinot Grigio

87 FRANZ HAAS Pinot Grigio Kris Alto Adige White 1994 **$10.00** Smoky, herbal aromas give way to polished flavors of mineral, pear and light toast in this elegant, harmonious white. It's subtle but lively, with a pleasant hint of spritz. A value for an Italian white, and it's made for food.

87 PETER ZEMMER Pinot Grigio Alto Adige 1995 **$10.00** This Italian white will wake up your taste buds. A crisp texture gives way to round flavors of pear and almond, but the citrus streak carries all the way through this balanced, refreshing wine. All that for so few dollars.

86 PAGGIO Pinot Grigio Alto Adige 1994 **$8.00** Expressive and distinctive. Unusual smoky and herbal aromas carry through on the ripe, yet firm, palate. It's clean and long. Not typical but worth a try.

85 CASA GIRELLI Pinot Grigio Trentino i Mesi 1995 **$9.00** Good varietal character in this lively white, offering fresh herbal and citrus flavors and vibrant acidity. It gets the juices flowing.

84 BOLLINI Pinot Grigio Grave del Friuli Reserve Selection 1994 **$8.00** Fresh in aroma, figgy in flavor, fruity enough to be satisfying, yet on the light side in body and texture.

84 BORGO MAGREDO Pinot Grigio Grave del Friuli 1994 **$8.00** Pungent herbal and smoky aromas give character to this white. It turns a bit softer on the palate, finishing in almond and light honey tones.

84 MALPAGA Pinot Grigio Trentino 1994 **$10.00** A mouth-filling texture and rather ripe pear flavors make this a full-bodied, well-made white wine. Can handle the Chardonnay role before or during the meal.

84 TIEFENBRUNNER Pinot Grigio Alto Adige 1994 **$10.00** Though lean, this clean white has good grip, with firm acidity and lingering flavors of lemon and hazelnut. A refreshing wine for food.

83 BORGO DELLE ROSE Pinot Grigio Grave del Friuli 1994 **$9.00** A deep gold color and butter-vanilla flavors make this taste barrel-aged. It's different, but could use more lively fruit flavors to back up the full body.

82 CANTINE MEZZACORONA Pinot Grigio Trentino 1995 **$8.00** Bright, fresh and lively, if light and rather watery in flavor.

82 MONTRESOR Pinot Grigio La Colombaia Valdadige White 1994 **$10.00** Mineral and citrus flavors give this white backbone; apple notes and a hint of butter provide roundness. It's an up-front wine for quaffing now.

81 LAGARIA Pinot Grigio 1994 **$6.50** Earthy, smoky and herbal, this white is rich and round, but isn't showing much fruit. It gets more interesting on the finish; try with food. ✪

81 SANTI Pinot Grigio Vigneto Sortesele Trentino White 1994 **$10.00** Fleshy and soft, with mineral, herb and light earthy flavors, this has good weight for a northern Italian white, but lacks fruit concentration and disappears on the finish.

80 CANALETTO Pinot Grigio delle Tre Venezie Vino da Tavola-Northeast White 1994 **$6.00** Smooth, light-bodied and has a soft texture. Offers light melon flavors and a short finish. ✪

80 COLLAVINI Pinot Grigio 1994 **$9.00** Sweet vanilla aromas are pleasant, but that's about the only flavor, except for hints of grapefruit. It's clean, very firm and refreshing, though.

80 COSI Pinot Grigio Valdadige 1993 **$10.00**
Age has softened and blurred this ripe, round wine.
Hints of honey and grilled nuts are pleasant, but the
fruit is fading without a firm backbone of acidity.

80 FONTANA CANDIDA Pinot Grigio 1994
$5.00 A simple white that goes down easy, this is
light and crisp, showing pear and almond notes and an
herbal finish. Best as an apéritif.

80 FURLAN CASTELCOSA Pinot Grigio
Castelcosa 1994 **$10.00** Exotic! Honey, pineapple
and hard candy flavors give this wine more personality than appeal. Firm acidity holds it together, but
there's little sense of grape variety or terroir.

80 LA MARCA Pinot Grigio Veneto 1994 **$6.00**
The refreshment value is high here, but there's not
enough flavor to keep your interest for long. It's firm,
clean and neutral. ○

Soave

84 ANSELMI Soave Classico Superiore San
Vincenzo 1994 **$9.00** Butter and honey flavors
overlay the pear and banana in this Soave. It has intensity and some length, adding a sweet, smoky finish.

84 GUERRIERI-RIZZARDI Soave Classico
Costeggiola 1994 **$9.00** A light and slighty sweet
tasting white with appealing peach flavors and a hint
of apricot and spice. Serve well-chilled.

82 GUERRIERI-RIZZARDI Soave Classico 1994 **$8.00** Buttery aromas and flavors with some green apple mixed in. It has character, but ends up a bit cloying on the finish.

80 CECILIA BERETTA Soave Classico Terre di Brognoligo 1993 **$8.00** Honey and vanilla flavors are appealing at first but then a bit cloying in this soft white. Coconut and floral notes add some interest.

Other White

88 NEIRANO Gavi 1994 **$10.00** A Gavi that offers something extra. This has great spicy aromas along with honey and baked apple flavors that linger on the finish. A firm, lively and full-bodied Italian white.

85 BORGO MAGREDO Sauvignon Grave del Friuli 1994 **$8.00** Grapefruit and herbal aromas are true to the varietal, and on the palate this is clean, fruity and refreshing. Well made in the Loire style.

84 BORGO MAGREDO Tocai Friulano Grave del Friuli 1994 **$7.50** Flavors of mandarin orange, honey and herb mingle in this soft, appealing white. It's not big, but has enough acidity to keep it lively.

84 PETER ZEMMER Gewürztraminer Alto Adige 1995 **$10.00** Rose petals and spice flow from this rich, round wine, with enough lemony acidity to keep it food-friendly. Distinctive and intriguing.

84 ZENATO Bianco di Custoza Sole dl Garda 1994 **$10.00** A wine with some punch to it; has good apple, unripe pear and some honey flavors. The finish is crisp, with a touch of almond.

84 ZENATO Lugana San Benedetto White 1994 **$10.00** Well-structured with good acidity and plenty of body. Tastes of fig and honey with a touch of spice. Pleasant and satisfying.

82 CARRETTA Bianco del Poggio 1993 **$9.00** An aggressive, toasty flavor dominates this medium-bodied white. There's enough acidity for balance, but not much fruit, finishing with a sweet, vanilla note.

81 LUIGI CALISSANO Villa Meriggi Gavi 1994 **$10.00** A sturdy Gavi with some depth and length to the melony, earthy flavors.

81 LAMBERTI Bianco di Custoza Orchidea Platino 1994 **$10.00** A slightly resinous white with an astringent finish. Piney and appley flavors dominate this medium-bodied wine, which also ends up quite dry as well.

BLUSH

83 SCARLATTA Montepulciano d'Abruzzo Cerasuolo 1993 **$4.00** A chalky character is the common theme here, but there is enough cherry and vibrant acidity to balance it. Austere, yet with plenty of personality.

SPARKLING

86 TOSTI Asti Spumante NV **$9.00** A sweet, spicy, minty, smooth-textured bubbly with a refreshing balance and distinctive flavors. A very good example of the style.

85 CINZANO Asti Spumante NV **$9.00** Pretty orange and spice aromas carry through on the soft and foamy palate. Enough acidity balances the sweetness, making this a light, pleasant apéritif or dessert wine that's well priced. ✪

80 CA' DE MONTE Moscato d'Asti NV **$8.00** Sweet, honeyed and herbaceous, with extremely youthful flavors, like just-pressed grape juice. Appealingly fresh and fruity, but simple.

Portugal

BY KIM MARCUS

Portugal is fast securing a place for itself on the short list of the world's great wine values. We're not talking Port, though. Instead, it is Portugal's red table wines that offer some of the best bargains. Good wines priced at $6 and under are common.

Most Portuguese wines are made out of native grape varieties; at their best, these wines are fruity and ripe. Traditionally, many Portuguese table wines were subjected to extended aging. This practice survives today in wines with the "garrafeira" designation, which denotes extended aging in wood vats and in the bottle. Many wineries have abandoned this style because of the deadening effect it can have on fruit flavors, though many good to very good garrafeiras are made.

Some of the best and most widely available Portuguese table wines today come from the Douro and Dão appellations. The Douro may be best known for its Port vineyards, but it is home to high-quality table wines as well.

In the Dão, situated in hilly country south of the Douro, the wines have benefited greatly from Portugal's 1986 entry into the Common Market. Before that time, government control of several large cooperatives in the region meant that quality was sacrificed for quantity. Growers were paid for bringing in the biggest harvest possible, and that made for flat-tasting wines. Now, many of the region's wineries are replanting vineyards with an eye to lower yields and higher quality, and are concentrating on a traditional grape variety of the region, Touriga Nacional.

The Alentejo region of southern Portugal also offers good to very good wines. The best taste something like a rich Beaujolais, with a jammy aroma and a lingering, fruity finish.

Most wines now on the market are from the 1992, 1993, and 1994 vintages, though older garrafeira selections are available.

Kim Marcus is assistant managing editor of Wine Spectator.

Most Reliable Values

These wines have proven to be of consistently good quality, year in and year out. Even if a particular vintage is not reviewed here, you may purchase these wines with confidence.

RED WINES

Carvalho, Ribeira & Ferreira Ribatejo Serradayres

Caves Aliança Beiras Galeria Cabernet Sauvignon

Caves Aliança Douro Foral Garrafeira

Caves Dom Teodosio Dão Cardeal

Cooperativa Reguengos De Monsaraz

Sogrape Alentejo Vinha do Monte

Sogrape Dão Duque de Viseu

Sogrape Douro Mateus Signature

Sogrape Douro Reserva

How to Read a
Portuguese Wine Label

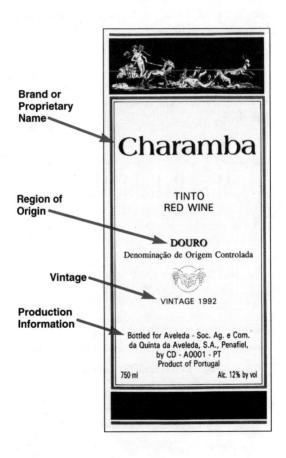

**Brand or
Proprietary
Name**

Charamba

TINTO
RED WINE

**Region of
Origin**

DOURO
Denominação de Origem Controlada

Vintage

VINTAGE 1992

**Production
Information**

Bottled for Aveleda - Soc. Ag. e Com.
da Quinta da Aveleda, S.A., Penafiel,
by CD - A0001 - PT
Product of Portugal

750 ml   Alc. 12% by vol

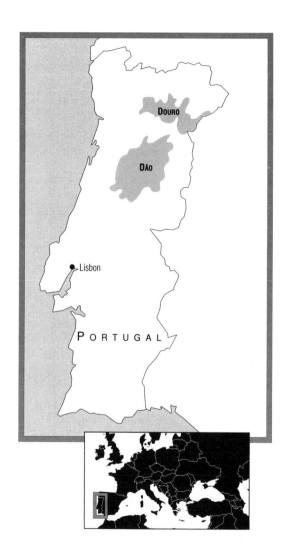

Red

Red

87 SOGRAPE Dão Duque de Viseu 1992 **$9.00**
A rich and deep Portuguese red that gives you lively
plum flavor, supported by coffee and chocolate notes,
good concentration and ripe tannins. It's fresh and
more complex than most of its peers. Drinkable now
or through 2000. ✪

85 COOPERATIVA REGUENGOS DE MON-
SARAZ Reguengos 1994 **$5.00** Luscious, featur-
ing loads of exuberant blackberry and blueberry flavors framed by clove and cinnamon notes. Adds a
touch of richness on the finish. A great bargain of a
Portuguese red. ✪

85 SOGRAPE Alentejo Vinha do Monte 1992
$9.00 Here's a bruiser. Deeply colored, highly
extracted, tannic and robust, showing some plum,
prune and tobacco flavors. A good steak would tame
it, or perhaps another year in bottle.

85 SOGRAPE Douro Reserva 1992 **$10.00** Well
made, concentrated, firmly tannic and rich with ripe
black cherry flavor. Herb, vanilla and cedar notes
linger on the finish. Pleasant now, it should be better
in 1997.

84 CAVES DOM TEODOSIO Dão Cardeal 1991
$6.50 Medium-bodied and mature in taste, sporting
cherry and mineral flavors, smoky aroma and a slightly tannic finish. Drinkable now while it's still lively.

✪ = Widest availability (over 15,000 cases produced)

84 J.P. VINHOS Alentejo Tinto da Anfora 1991
$10.00 Solid and lively, dominated by good raspberry and blueberry flavors and a nice, spicy finish.
Drinkable now.

84 QUINTA DE MATO MIRANDA Ribatejo 1992
$5.50 Ripe, fairly rich and rustic, offering plenty of
tannins. Flavors are dominated by cherry and coffee,
inserting a shot of licorice on the finish. Drinkable
now.

83 CARVALHO, RIBEIRA & FERREIRA Ribatejo
Serradayres 1993 **$6.50** Starts off lean but builds
intensity with good blueberry, raspberry and cherry
flavors. Medium-bodied and delicious, adding a nice
touch of spice on aftertaste. Ready to drink now.

83 CAVES ALIANÇA Cabernet Sauvignon Beiras
Galeria 1994 **$9.00** A punchy Cabernet offering
plum and herb flavors and firm, tannic backbone. It's
concentrated, if somewhat rustic. Drinkable now.

83 J.P. VINHOS Alentejo Herdade de Santa
Marta 1993 **$9.00** Straightforward, fairly ripe plum,
raspberry and sweet cherry flavors linger on the finish. A good quaff.

83 QUINTA DA LAGOALVA Ribatejo Cima 1992
$9.00 Rustic, delivering plenty of hearty game, earth
and ripe plum flavors. The finish kicks in some tobacco and cedary notes. Simple and satisfying.

83 QUINTA DE PARROTES Alenquer 1992
$7.00 Bright cherry flavor animates this round, fresh
red, adding black pepper accents and light tannins. It
has personality, if not much weight.

82 ADEGA COOPERTIVA Alentejo Vila Morena 1994 **$5.00** Jammy and fruity, offering good blackberry and blueberry flavors, a touch of richness, some nice, spicy shadings and lively acidity.

82 CAVES ALIANÇA Douro Foral 1992 **$8.00** Soft, velvety, sweet cherry and plum flavors. It has an earthy streak running through the middle, but it's still enjoyable. Drinkable now.

82 CASA DE SANTAR Dão Reserva 1992 **$10.00** Nice shades of vanilla and spice, lots of raspberry and cherry flavors and crisp finish.

82 CAVES DOM TEODOSIO Cartaxo Quinta do Bairro Falcão 1993 **$7.50** Fleshy black cherry and light earth flavors, soft and round. Straightforward but drinking well now.

82 CAVES DOM TEODOSIO Tomar Quinta de S. João Batista 1992 **$7.50** Mature and soft, this offers raisin, smoke and light herbal flavors in a supple, spicy package. Not rich but sweetly agreeable.

82 ESPORAO Reguengos Monte Velho 1992 **$7.00** This shows supple, fleshy texture and raisin, spice and light tobacco flavors. It's straightforward and accessible.

82 QUINTA DE SAES Dão 1992 **$10.00** There's a nice spiciness here, reminiscent of white pepper. Smooth, supple and round, delivering plum and dried cherry flavors which linger on the finish.

81 SOGRAPE Dão Grão Vasco 1992 **$5.00**
Light-bodied but firm, this brisk red offers cherry,
smoky and light herbal flavors. It's well knit and a
good accompaniment for food. ✪

80 SOGRAPE Douro Mateus Signature 1992
$6.00 Good dried cherry and earthy flavors and aromas.
A pleasant, fully mature red that's ready to drink now. ✪

WHITE

85 MANUEL SALVADOR PEREIRA Vinho Verde
Alvarinho Dom Salvador 1994 **$10.00** Has excel-
lent body and flavor for a normally lean white type.
Combines fresh, floral, appley notes with crisp acidity
and a nicely bitter finish that lingers.

82 CAVES DA CERCA Vinho Verde Tâmega
1993 **$5.00** A good seafood wine. Dry and tart, but
carrying enough apple and lemon flavors to make it
lively and refreshing. ✪

82 QUINTA DO MINHO Vinha Verde 1994 **$7.00**
Light and lean white, distinctive in flavor, showing
crisp apple and grapefruit accents. Spritzy enough to
keep it lively.

81 AVELEDA Vinho Verde NV **$6.00** Robust
white, generous in flavor, quite firm with acidity and
spritzy in texture. ✪

80 CAVES ALIANÇA Vinho Verde NV **$5.00**
Light, fresh, apple-flavored and slightly spritzy in
texture. Good, simple white.

DESSERT

Port

82 DOW Tawny Port NV **$10.00** Simple, plummy,
peppery, fruitcake aromas and flavors, medium body
and sweetness and fruity finish.

South Africa

By James Suckling

Following a change in government in 1994 and an
aggressive policy of expanding exports, South Africa
has emerged as a solid source of quality wines at reasonable prices. Images of vineyards growing in arid
grasslands dotted with zebras and giraffes may come
to mind when someone speaks of South Africa; in
fact, most of its quality vineyards are located in or
near the seaside city of Cape Town, and benefit from
the cooling influence of its maritime climate.

For the most part, South African wine nomenclature resembles that of the United States. Wines are
usually made from a predominant grape; Chardonnay,
Sauvignon Blanc and Cabernet Sauvignon are
extremely popular and produce the best wines.
Nonetheless, the variety with the largest plantings is
Chenin Blanc, called "Steen" locally, which can produce everything from crisp, clean dry white wines to
oaky brandy. Another favorite grape is Pinotage,
which is a cross between the refined Pinot Noir and
the coarse Cinsault. It can make light and refreshing
rosés as well as powerful, long-lived reds.

The selection of South African wines available
in America remains rather limited, although many
producers in such quality regions as Constantia, Paarl,
and Stellenbosch have their eyes on the U.S. market.

Varietal red wines made from Shiraz (also known
as Syrah), Cabernet Sauvignon and Merlot are among
the best values from South Africa. They offer flavors
that are subtly different from their counterparts in

other countries. Pinotage is a grape variety found only in South Africa and it also can make unique, value-priced red wines.

James Suckling is European bureau chief of Wine Spectator.

Most Reliable Values

These wines have proven to be of consistently good quality, year in and year out. Even if a particular vintage is not reviewed here, you may purchase these wines with confidence.

RED WINES

Backsberg Shiraz Paarl

Springbok Pinotage Coastal Region

Swartland Winery Cabernet Sauvignon Swartland Region

Swartland Winery Merlot Swartland Region

Swartland Winery Pinotage Swartland Region

How to Read a South African Wine Label

Brand or Proprietary Name

Grape Variety

Producer or Estate

Region of Origin

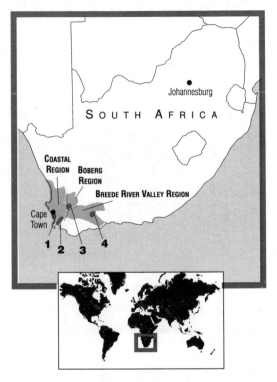

1. Constantia   **3.** Paarl

2. Stellenbosch   **4.** Robertson

RED

Pinotage

87 SPRINGBOK Pinotage Coastal Region 1993 **$6.50** Serious, tannic, engaging Pinotage boasting depth and complexity in the cherry and strawberry flavors and a dry, firm texture. Lingering finish, too. Drinkable now through 1998.

85 GOOD HOPE WINES Pinotage Paarl 1994 **$9.00** A solid, serious red showing touches of pepper accenting the cherry-strawberry flavors. Moderately tannic, very dry, nicely smooth.

84 CAPE INDABA Pinotage Coastal Region 1995 **$9.00** Extremely bright, fruity and clean. A young red for enjoying now, featuring ample strawberry flavor, soft texture and clear finish.

83 SWARTLAND WINERY Pinotage Swartland Region 1995 **$9.00** A nouveau-style red, quite like Beaujolais, offering lots of jammy and ripe fruit flavors, soft tannins and lingering finish.

Shiraz and Shiraz Blend

85 BACKSBERG Shiraz Paarl 1992 **$10.00** A solid, flavorful, gamy-tasting and exotic red offering firm tannins and raspberry and pepper notes. Turns rather lean and dry on the finish.

✪ = Widest availability (over 15,000 cases produced)

85 FAIRVIEW ESTATE Shiraz/Merlot Paarl 1991
$8.00 Bright aromas of black cherry and mint give
way to round, soft plum, cherry and chocolate flavors.
It's still lively and very accessible. Drink now, while
the fruit is fresh.

83 FAIRVIEW ESTATE Shiraz Paarl 1992 **$8.00**
Good to drink now. A jammy, medium-bodied red
showing smoky aromas and raspberry tones. Richly
flavored, but light in tannins and short on the finish.

81 NEETHLINGSHOF Shiraz Stellenbosch
1992 **$10.00** Heavy, brooding, full-bodied, smoky,
almost bitter; coffee and meaty notes are more prominent than the blackberry flavors. Drinkable now.

80 SWARTLAND WINERY Shiraz Swartland
Region 1992 **$9.00** A hint of greenness combines
with nice mint and vanilla character. Medium in body;
enough fruit flavor, plus light tannins so you can drink
it now.

Other Red

87 SORGVLIET Grand Vin Rouge Stellenbosch
1992 **$7.00** An intriguing earthy, spicy aroma marks
this full-bodied, moderately tannic red. Reminiscent
of Cabernet Sauvignon, adding some nice oaky
accents to the ripe cherry and plum flavors.

87 SWARTLAND WINERY Merlot Swartland Region 1995 **$10.00** Lushly textured and opulent, featuring deep, dark color and rich fruit flavors generously accented with oak. Tempting to drink now for its exuberant fruitiness, but may improve through 1999.

86 DROSTDY-HOF Merlot Coastal Region 1992 **$10.00** Plums, spices, touches of herbs-this shows good varietal character in a fresh, balanced red. It's polished and has enough tannin to stand up to food. Drinkable now.

85 SWARTLAND WINERY Cabernet Sauvignon Swartland Region 1993 **$9.00** Solid, fruity-tasting; enjoyable cherry and black currant last from first whiff through the finish. Has supple texture, mild tannins and accents of vanilla from oak aging. Drink now.

84 NEETHLINGSHOF Cabernet Sauvignon Stellenbosch 1990 **$10.00** Sturdy, solid style of Cabernet that packs in plenty of ripe currant and cherry flavor; little oak influence. Tight and firm in texture and a tannic grip on the finish.

WHITE

Chardonnay

82 SPRINGBOK Chardonnay Coastal Region 1995 **$7.00** An obvious style, sporting oak and caramel flavors and a touch of lemon and citrus. Simple, but tasty with good acidity. ✪

82 STELLENZICHT Chardonnay Stellenbosch 1993 **$7.00** Attractive toast and butter aromas give way to maturing flavors of pear and toast and an earthy, leesy finish. This ambitious effort still has appeal.

82 THE AFRICA COLLECTION Chardonnay Stellenbosch 1992 **$6.00** Made in a crisp, lean style, this has modest appley, buttery flavors and comparatively light texture. Charming and well balanced.

81 LANZERAC Chardonnay Stellenbosch 1994 **$8.50** Light and crisp in style, this offers simple apple and nutmeg flavors. It's clean and easy to drink.

Other White

85 WELMOED WINERY Sauvignon Blanc Stellenbosch 1994 **$8.00** Crisp and clean. Characteristic grassy aromas and dry, juicy flavors remind us of a good French Sancerre. Should be versatile at the table.

84 NEETHLINGSHOF Riesling Stellenbosch Weisser Riesling 1993 **$10.00** Crisp and clean, this combines racy acidity and tropical fruitiness accented by spicy vanilla notes. It's vivid and refreshing.

84 NEETHLINGSHOF Riesling Stellenbosch Weisser Riesling Off Dry 1993 **$10.00** Big-boned and sturdy, showing melon and herbal flavors, fine intensity and acidity. Not much sweetness. Good for food, though lacking clear Riesling character.

Spain

By Thomas Matthews

Spain has long been proud of its national traditions, and its wineries have staunchly resisted the international style of oaky Chardonnays and tannic Cabernets. This Mediterranean country's top values continue to be made with native grape varieties in traditional styles. They reward exploration by adventurous wine drinkers.

The most successful wines in every price category are red, primarily those made from the Tempranillo grape, which dominates the regions of Rioja, Ribera del Duero, Navarra and Toro. Rioja, traditionally the most prestigious Spanish red wine region, now faces plenty of competition, especially in the $6 to $10 price range. Cabernet Sauvignon has begun to make an appearance, often blended with Tempranillo, while obscure local grape varieties contribute to the distinctive character of wines from Penedés, Priorato and Somontano.

Most wineries offer reds in four quality levels, which correspond to the amount of aging (in wooden barrels or in bottle) the wines receive before release; in order of increasing age (and price), they are "sin crianza," "crianza," "reserva" and "gran reserva." For the best values and the freshest fruit, look for "crianza" and "reserva" level red wines. The 1991 and '94 vintages are the best currently on the market.

Sparkling wines, made by the classic Champagne methode but using indigenous grapes, also provide good value. Called *cava*, these come primarily from the Penedés region near Barcelona. Don't worry too much about special designations or vintages; the non-vintage cuvées offer the best value and a hearty, straightforward taste perfect for parties or punches.

Whites are hit or miss in Spain. White Riojas and Ruedas, made from Viura, are fresh and clean, while "reservas," aged in American oak, are voluptuous and herb-scented. Spanish Chardonnays and other white varietals have few advantages over those from other countries, but a few indigenous grapes make distinctive wines from northern regions such as Penedés and Galicia.

Thomas Matthews is New York bureau chief of Wine Spectator.

Most Reliable Values

These wines have proven to be of consistently good quality, year in and year out. Even if a particular vintage is not reviewed here, you may purchase these wines with confidence.

RED WINES
Bodegas Martinez Bujanda Rioja Conde de
   Valdemar Crianza
Bodegas Montecillo Rioja Viña Cumbrero Crianza
Jaume Serra Penedès Crianza
Marques de Grinon
Rene Barbier Merlot Penedès Mediterranean Select

WHITE WINE
Marques de Caceres Rioja

BLUSH WINES
Marques de Caceras Rioja Rosé

SPARKLING WINES
Freixenet Brut Cava Carta Nevada NV
Paul Cheneau Brut Cava Blanc de Blancs NV

How to Read a
Spanish Wine Label

**Region of
Origin**

Importer

**Producer
& Estate
Information**

**Brand or
Proprietary
Name**

1. Rueda
2. Ribera del Duero
3. Rioja
4. Navarra
5. Priorato
6. Penedès
7. Jerez

RED

Rioja

88 MARQUES DE GRINON Rioja 1994 **$10.00**
Pretty vanilla and berry flavors are soft and lush in
this drink-me-now red. It's bright and lively, and finishes with nice spicy notes. Delicacy and vivacity are
its strong points. ✪

86 BODEGAS BERBERANA Rioja Tempranillo
Dragon Label 1994 **$10.00** Ripe and round, with
plenty of sweet vanilla oak flavors. Has enough cherry
and light plum to keep it balanced. Very pleasant,
though not much structure, so drink up. ✪

85 BODEGAS AGE Rioja Siglo Reserva 1986
$10.00 Holding up well: silky, traditional, showing
coffee, spice and raisin flavors in a lean, soft frame. It
matches well with food and has enough elegance to be
enjoyed on its own. Drinkable now.

84 BODEGAS FAUSTINO MARTINEZ Rioja
Faustino V Reserva 1991 **$10.00** Firm and harmo-
nious, this rich red offers plum, tobacco and light
earth notes in a rather somber package that's best
accompanied by food. Drinkable now.

84 BODEGAS MONTECILLO Rioja Viña
Cumbrero Crianza 1991 **$7.00** A big Rioja. Dark
color, full, firm tannins and deep notes of currant,
coffee and chocolate give this red presence.
Drinkable now.

✪ = Widest availability (over 15,000 cases produced)

83 BODEGAS SENDA GALIANA Rioja Reserva 1989 **$10.00** Elegant in the traditional style. Flavors of berries, tea and vanilla mingle in this firm but light-bodied red. A nice match with light dishes, but drinkable now.

83 RICAVI Rioja Crianza 1991 **$8.00** Silky and charming, if light, this offers typical strawberry, tea and vanilla flavors, fresh and lean, achieving some intensity. Drinkable now.

82 BODEGAS BERBERANA Tempranillo Crianza Rioja 1991 **$9.00** Traditional style Rioja, smooth and lean, with cola, herb and raisin flavors. Could be fresher, but it has character. Light and drinkable now. ✪

82 BODEGAS MARTINEZ BUJANDA Conde de Valdemar Crianza Rioja 1992 **$10.00** A round wine with light tannins, plenty of vanilla and ripe plum and licorice flavors. It's soft enough for drinking now.

81 BODEGAS BRETON Rioja Loriñon Crianza 1991 **$10.00** Raspberry and vanilla aromas and flavors are appealing, but this red is a bit tart and tannic, lacking ripeness. Better accompanying food. Drinkable now. ✪

81 BODEGAS SIERRA CANTABRIA Rioja Codice 1993 **$7.00** There's some berry flavor here, with accents of vanilla and spice, but it's diluted with a drying finish. It might soften with food.

81 BODEGAS SIERRA CANTABRIA Rioja 1991 **$8.00** Pleasant spice and black cherry flavors are still fresh, but firm tannins close down on the finish. It has life ahead of it, and may soften with food.

81 RICAVI Rioja 1994 **$6.00** Soft and fruity, medium body, light tannins and just enough spice to give it interest. Easy drinking now.

80 BODEGAS BERBERANA Tempranillo d'Avalos Rioja 1994 **$8.00** Deep color, velvet texture, with flavors of smoke, tar and ripe blackberries. This seems more like Beaujolais than Rioja. Pleasant enough, but it's soft and a bit flabby. ✪

Other Red

86 VINAS DEL VERO Merlot Somontano Saint Marc 1993 **$8.00** Fruit, fruit and more fruit. Loads of blueberry and blackberry flavors with a good structure and enough tannins to let it age. Nicely concentrated with a lingering, chocolately finish. Better in 1997.

84 BODEGAS GUELBENZU Navarra 1994 **$10.00** Harmonious, firm and ripe, offering black cherry, spice and light herbal flavors in a well-knit, though not showy, package. A good wine with food; drinkable now.

84 RENE BARBIER Merlot Penedès Mediterranean Select 1992 **$7.00** Sweet vanilla oak dominates this round, supple red, also showing pleasant black cherry flavor and light coffee accents. It's quite rich, if a bit simple.

83 BODEGAS AGAPITO RICO Monastrell Jumilla 1994 **$6.00** Firm and meaty, adding game and licorice flavors to the core of blackberry. It's got some concentration, but could use more liveliness.

83 MARQUES DE GRINON Castilla y Leon Durius 1993 **$9.00** Lively, packed with ripe plum, blackberry and coffee flavors, adding soft tannins and bright acidity. It's clean and lingers on the finish. Drinkable now. ✪

83 JAUME SERRA Penedès Crianza 1992 **$7.00** Tobacco and light barnyard aromas give way to a round, soft texture and ripe flavors of plum, herb and vanilla. It's generous, straightforward and drinkable now. ✪

83 TAJA Jumilla 1994 **$5.50** Firm and juicy, spice and earth notes accenting the black cherry flavor. It's straightforward but balanced and bright.

83 VINAS DEL VERO Somontano Saint Marc Duque de Azara Crianza 1991 **$9.00** Solid, fresh, ripe fruit, mingling black cherry, herbal and chocolate flavors with good backbone and a clean finish. Somewhat rustic, but good food accompaniment. ✪

83 VINICOLA NAVARRA Navarra Las Campanas Crianza 1991 **$7.00** Sweet vanilla and raspberry flavors are enticing in this soft, maturing red, but ultimately seem somewhat simple. Still, a pleasant quaff. ✪

82 BODEGA ROMERO Navarra Via Corel 1993 **$6.00** Clean and refreshing, silky, offering black cherry, licorice and spice flavors, bright acidity and light tannins. Good for food.

82 BODEGAS AGAPITO RICO Monastrell Jumilla Carchelo 1995 **$8.00** Plum flavors have a slight, pleasant, bitter note in this firm, ripe red. It's somewhat alcoholic for balance, but fruit lingers on the finish.

82 FARINA Zamora Gran Peromato 1990 **$6.00**
This smooth, solid red isn't showy, but it offers ripe, chunky flavors of plums and prunes, adding hints of vanilla and herbs and firm tannins.

82 JAUME SERRA Tempranillo Penedès 1993 **$5.00** Fleshy and supple, this bright red offers pleasant raspberry and light herbal flavors, adding just enough grip to balance with food. Drinkable now. ✪

81 BODEGA ROMERO Navarra La Cruceta 1994 **$7.00** This understated red is balanced and clean yet not showing much fruit now, delivering light herbal, orange and spice notes. Pleasant but not memorable.

81 VINAS DEL VERO Somontano Saint Marc Estate Reserva Especial 1991 **$9.00** A solid, rustic red offering ripe flavors of plums and blackberries. It's almost jammy, but firm tannins give it grip.

80 RENE BARBIER Cabernet Sauvignon Penedès Mediterranean Select 1990 **$7.00** Coffee and herbal flavors predominate in this chewy red. It's round, has some grip and a nice, fruity sweetness on the palate, but lacks focus. Drinkable now.

80 CASTILLO PERELADA Cabernet Sauvignon Empordà-Costa Brava 1991 **$10.00** Smooth and light mix of herbal and raisin flavors that finishes a bit dry. Drinkable with food but don't wait.

80 CASTILLO PERELADA Empordà-Costa Brava Reserva 1990 **$9.00** Mature, smooth and sweet, showing raisin, brown sugar and light herbal flavors, then turning dry on the finish. Drinkable now.

80 SALVADOR POVEDA Monastrell Alicante Tinto Reserva 1989 **$8.00** A quaffable red showing berry, raisin, orange peel and walnut flavors. This is still quite lively but wants drinking now. ✪

White

84 MARQUES DE CACERES Rioja 1993 **$7.00** Grapefruit and herbal flavors are refreshing. Clean, crisp and has enough body to stand up to food. Balanced and has some richness.

82 MARQUES DE RISCAL Rueda 1994 **$8.00** Clean and fresh, this offers a streak of tropical fruit to add interest to its basic white wine character.

81 VINAS DEL VERO Saint Marc Estate Duque de Azara Somontano 1994 **$8.00** Round and soft, with light herbal and apple flavors; this is dry and clean. Fine with food. ✪

80 FARINA Colegiata Toro 1994 **$7.00** Clean, well-balanced, almost neutral in flavor, but light pear and hazelnut flavors linger on the finish. Simple but well-made.

80 VINAS DEL VERO Chardonnay Somontano Barrel Fermented Reserve Saint Marc Estate 1994 **$9.00** An overenthusiastic dose of oak gives this wine aromas of white chocolate and black coffee, while a thick texture and flavors of vanilla and butter show on the palate. Enough melon flavor peeps through to keep it pleasant, but it's for barrel lovers.

BLUSH

86 MARQUES DE CACERES Rioja Rosé 1993
$7.00 A perennial good value for the red and white,
and this rosé stays true to form. From the strawberry,
cherry, melon and spice flavors to the dry finish, this
is loaded with personality. The vibrant acidity should
make this a versatile match with food. **✪**

83 VINICOLA NAVARRA Navarra Las
Campanas 1993 **$7.00** Lean, dry and spicy, ending
with notes of herbs and watermelon. A firm, dry style
that begs for Mediterranean salads or seafood.

82 VINA VALORIA Rioja 1993 **$10.00** Raspberry
and kirsch aromas are assertive and promising, but a
heavy texture dulls the flavors. The concentration
shows on the finish.

80 BODEGA ROMERO Navarra Malón de
Echaide 1993 **$7.00** Some herbal, raspberry notes
beg for attention underneath its tough, dry structure.

SPARKLING

86 SEGURA VIUDAS Brut Cava Reserve NV
$7.00 Tastes flavorful and complex, is rich in texture and
long on the finish. Has powerful fruit and good balance.

85 JAUME SERRA Brut Cava Cristalino NV
$7.50 A full-flavored, assertive Spanish sparkler that
starts with toasty, spicy aromas, then wraps its nutty,
fruity flavors in a rich texture. Lingers nicely on the
finish. Lots of character for this price range.

84 FREIXENET Brut Cava Carta Nevada NV **$7.00** Generously flavored and soft-textured, with apple and honey aromas, frothy bubbles and a mineral-like accent.

84 FREIXENET Brut Rosé Cava NV **$10.00** Clean-tasting, fresh and well-balanced. Easy to drink, with an appealing, light and foamy texture.

84 MONT-MARÇAL Cava 1993 **$10.00** A nicely perfumed, smooth-textured sparkling wine with subtle fruit, spice and nut flavors. On the soft, light-bodied side and easy to enjoy.

84 SEGURA VIUDAS Brut Cava Aria NV **$10.00** A mini-Champagne: Has the enticing doughy, spicy aromas and solid fruit flavors expected in a sparkling wine.

83 PAUL CHENEAU Brut Cava Blanc de Blancs NV **$8.00** A good, sound clean-tasting bottle of bubbly with modest fruit flavors and a smooth texture.

83 SUMARROCA Brut Cava NV **$8.00** A light, charming sparkling wine with applelike flavors, a soft texture and short finish.

81 SUMARROCA Extra Brut Cava NV **$8.00** Very fruity, crisp direct style of sparkling wine with lots of citrus flavors and a dry, firm feel.

U.S.A.

BY HARVEY STEIMAN

As wines such as Chardonnay, Cabernet Sauvignon, Merlot and Pinot Noir have become more popular, their prices have risen correspondingly, and searching for good values among them has become trickier. The lion's share of U.S.-made wine values comes in two basic areas: good wines made from less popular grape varieties, and well-made, mass-produced wines from big wineries.

Traditionally, the best buys were generic, blended wines—those that used to be labeled Chablis or Burgundy, and are now usually simply called table wine. More recently, some of the largest wineries in California and Washington have also found success selling Chardonnays, Cabernets, and other prestigious varietals—that is, wines made entirely or mostly from the single grape variety named on the front label—at less than $10.

When carefully made, these wines represent excellent value. How do they do it? They use grapes from less-prominent regions, age the wine in barrels already used for expensive wines, or blend judiciously to make good wine at a fair price.

Smart buyers also know that top-ranked Rieslings, Gewürztraminers, and to a lesser extent, Sauvignon Blancs, cannot command the prices Chardonnay can. These can be crowd-pleasing white wines, full of fruit flavor and personality, yet they have not thus far achieved the recognition they deserve.

Lesser-known wine regions often present some of the best values. Areas of California such as San Luis

Obispo and the Sierra Foothills lack the cachet of Napa and Sonoma, so their wines carry more appealing price tags. And vineyard land in Washington and Idaho is cheaper than land in California, which makes it possible for those states to price good wines attractively.

Unfortunately, the same does not hold true for wine regions in the eastern United States. Capricious weather makes it tough for good wineries in Virginia, New York and Texas to match the quality-to-price ratio California and Washington can achieve. Eastern wineries can turn out distinctive wines, but prices tend to be higher than similar-quality wines from the west.

You might also think that new-to-the U.S., relatively untested grape varieties would offer good values, but such is not the case. Recent enthusiasm in California for Rhône varieties (Syrah, Mourvèdre, Viognier) and Italian varieties (Sangiovese, Nebbiolo) has translated into interesting wines, but at high prices. Few cost less than $10, except for the occasional Grenache or Barbera.

Other less-celebrated wines can also qualify as good values, including Pinot Gris and Riesling from Oregon, Zinfandel and Chardonnay from Mendocino, Chenin Blanc and Lemberger from Washington, and Riesling from New York and Virginia. The secret to finding value in an American wine is to ignore pedigree and explore lesser-known regions and wines.

Harvey Steiman is editor at large of Wine Spectator.

Most Reliable Values

These wines have proven to be of consistently good quality, year in and year out. Even if a particular vintage is not reviewed here, you may purchase these wines with confidence.
(Note: Wines not designated otherwise are from California)

CABERNET SAUVIGNON/CABERNET BLENDS
Bandiera Cabernet Sauvignon
Columbia Crest Cabernet Sauvignon (Washington)
Dunnewood Cabernet Sauvignon Barrel Select
Hedges Cabernet-Merlot Columbia Valley
Hess Select Cabernet Sauvignon
J. Lohr Cabernet Sauvignon Cypress
Napa Ridge Cabernet Sauvignon
Parducci Cabernet Sauvignon
Paul Thomas Cabernet Merlot (Washington)

MERLOT
Columbia Crest Merlot (Washington)
Fetzer Merlot California Eagle Peak
J. Lohr Merlot California Cypress
Louis M. Martini Merlot
Napa Ridge Merlot

PINOT NOIR
Carneros Creek Pinot Noir Carneros Fleur de
  Carneros
Firesteed Pinot Noir (Oregon)
Louis M. Martini Pinot Noir
Napa Ridge Pinot Noir

continued on next page

Most Reliable Values *continued*

Pinot Noir *continued*

Napa Ridge Pinot Noir
Parducci Pinot Noir Mendocino County
Pepperwood Grove Pinot Noir
Tualatin Pinot Noir (Oregon)
Tualatin Pinot Noir Willamette Valley Barrel Aged
  (Oregon)
Villa Mt. Eden Pinot Noir Cellar Select

Syrah

R.H. Phillips Syrah California
McDowell Syrah Mendocino

Zinfandel

Beringer Zinfandel
Bogle Zinfandel
Chateau Souverain Zinfandel Dry Creek Valley
Round Hill Zinfandel Napa Valley
Sausal Zinfandel Alexander Valley
Seghesio Zinfandel Sonoma County
Villa Mt. Eden Zinfandel California Cellar Select

Other Red Wines

Bogle Petite Sirah
Bonny Doon Clos de Gilroy
Parducci Petite Sirah
Preston Gamay Beaujolais
Preston Gamay Beaujolais Dry Creek Valley

Chardonnay

Belvedere Chardonnay Sonoma County
Bridgeview Chardonnay Oregon Barrel Select
  (Oregon)
Columbia Crest Chardonnay (Washington)

Fetzer Chardonnay North Coast Barrel Select
Hess Select Chardonnay
Hogue Chardonnay (Washington)
Knudsen Erath Chardonnay (Oregon)
J. Lohr Chardonnay California Cypress
Louis M. Martini Chardonnay
Meridian Chardonnay Santa Barbara County
Navarro Chardonnay Mendocino
Taft Street Chardonnay Sonoma County
Vichon Chardonnay Coastal Selection
Villa Mt. Eden Chardonnay Cellar Select
Wente Bros. Chardonnay Seco Riva Ranch

CHENIN BLANC
Chappellet Chenin Blanc
Hogue Chenin Blanc Dry (Washington)

GEWÜRZTRAMINER
Claiborne & Churchill Gewürztraminer Alsatian
  Style Dry
Columbia Gewürztraminer (Washington)
Geyser Peak Gewürztraminer
Geyser Peak Gewürztraminer California

RIESLING
Bonny Doon Riesling California Pacific Rim
Chateau Ste. Michelle White Riesling Late Harvest
  Columbia Valley Chateau Reserve (Washington)
Claiborne & Churchill Riesling Alsatian Style Dry
Columbia Johannisberg Riesling (Washington)
Hermann J. Wiemer Johannisberg Riesling Finger
  Lakes Semi-Dry (New York)

continued on next page

Most Reliable Values *continued*

RIESLING *continued*
Dr. Konstantin Frank Johannisberg Riesling
  Finger Lakes Semi-Dry (New York)
Lamoreaux Landing Johannisberg Riesling (New York)
Tualatin White Riesling (Oregon)

SAUVIGNON BLANC/FUMÉ BLANC
Beaulieu Sauvignon Blanc Napa Valley
Bernardus Sauvignon Blanc Monterey County
Buena Vista Sauvignon Blanc Lake County
Chateau Souverain Sauvignon Blanc
Fetzer Fumé Blanc Mendocino County
Geyser Peak Sauvignon Blanc Sonoma County
Hogue Fumé Blanc (Washington)
Hogue Fumé Blanc Columbia Valley (Washington)
Murphy-Goode Fumé Blanc Alexander Valley
Voss Sauvignon Blanc

OTHER WHITE WINES
Columbia Sémillon (Washington)
Columbia Crest Sémillon (Washington)
Hogue Sémillon (Washington)

SPARKLING
Domaine Ste. Michelle Blanc de Blanc Columbia
  Valley

OTHER CATEGORIES
Beringer White Zinfandel (Blush)
Mirassou White Zinfandel (Blush)
Sutter Home Muscat Alexandria California
  (Dessert Wine)
Vendange White Zinfandel (Blush)

How to Read an American Wine Label

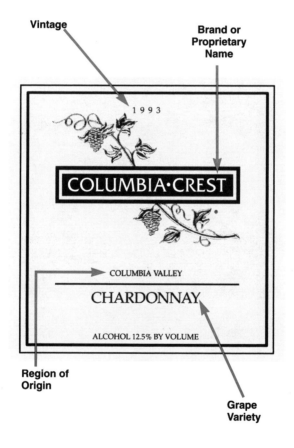

Vintage

Brand or Proprietary Name

1993

COLUMBIA·CREST

COLUMBIA VALLEY

CHARDONNAY

ALCOHOL 12.5% BY VOLUME

Region of Origin

Grape Variety

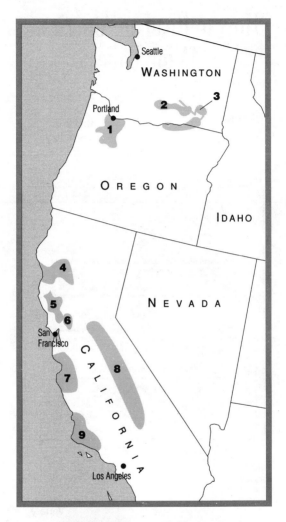

1. Willamette Valley
2. Yakima Valley
3. Columbia Valley
4. Mendocino & Lake Counties
5. Sonoma
6. Napa
7. Central Coast
8. Central Valley
9. South Central Coast

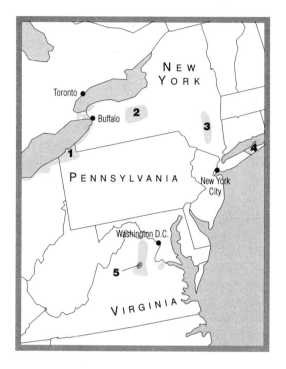

1. Lake Erie   4. Long Island
2. Finger Lakes   5. Monticello
3. Hudson Valley

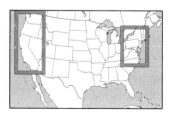

Red

Cabernet Blend

CALIFORNIA

80 MICHAEL SULLBERG Merlot Cab Cuvée Reserve Mount Veeder NV **$6.00** Light and airy, aiming for delicacy over power, modest in flavor, more beery fruit up front than on the finish.

WASHINGTON

87 POWERS Cabernet-Merlot Columbia Valley 1994 **$10.00** Bright, plummy flavors make this a lively blend, balancing its zesty fruit against a firm frame of fine tannin and some spiciness. Best in 1998.

84 PAUL THOMAS Cabernet-Merlot Washington 1994 **$9.50** Open-textured and plummy, a bit light on intensity but very pretty. Approachable now.

83 HEDGES Cabernet-Merlot Columbia Valley 1994 **$9.50** Light and velvety, as modest red berry and cedary flavors linger tentatively on the finish. Ready now. ✪

83 WASHINGTON HILLS Varietal Select Columbia Valley 1993 **$9.00** Lean and a little chewy, appealing cherry and tarry flavors showing on the finish.

✪ = Widest availability (over 15,000 cases produced)

Cabernet Sauvignon

CALIFORNIA

89 STONEHEDGE Cabernet Sauvignon Napa Valley Winemaker's Reserve 1992 **$10.00** Smooth and elegant, with a supple band of cherry, currant and raspberry flavors couched in light oak shadings. Finishes with firm, fine tannins. Needs until 1999 to show its best.

88 PARDUCCI Cabernet Sauvignon Mendocino County 1992 **$8.00** Not much on the nose from this California value wine, but it's ripe and chewy on the palate, concentrating its plum and black currant flavors in a thick, rich finish that lasts. Not too tannic, but should be better in 1998.

87 EXPRESSIONS Cabernet Sauvignon Napa Valley 1993 **$10.00** Ripe and harmonious, offering supple plum and cherry flavors and a dry, tannic finish. Tempting now at this price, but best to wait until 2000.

87 NAPA RIDGE Cabernet Sauvignon Central Coast 1992 **$8.00** Ripe and fruity, with a core of jammy black cherry and wild berry flavors that have a tannic edge. Needs only a little aging to enhance its value even more. ❂

87 NAPA RIDGE Cabernet Sauvignon North Coast Coastal Oak Barrel 1993 **$7.50** Has appealing spicy berry and toasty oak flavors that are pleasantly well proportioned. Another terrific value from this California winery. ❂

87 RUTHERFORD VINEYARDS Cabernet Sauvignon Napa Valley Rutherford Bench 1992 **$8.00** Smooth, supple and generous with its plum, berry, spice and vanilla flavors that keep weaving through . Tannins can use until 1998, but it's appealing now.

87 SEBASTIANI Cabernet Sauvignon Sonoma County 1992 **$10.00** Light and jammy, packing in plenty of raspberry and cola flavors that glide smoothly through the finish. Approachable now, best from 1997. ✪

85 BANDIERA Cabernet Sauvignon Napa Valley 1993 **$8.00** Pleasant for its ripe plum, spice and berry flavors and mild tannins. A light dash of oak adds interest in this value red. ✪

85 BOGLE Cabernet Sauvignon California 1993 **$6.50** Good flavor for the price. Simple and nicely focused currant and blackberry flavors echo nicely on the finish. Drinkable now.

85 CANYON ROAD Cabernet Sauvignon California 1993 **$6.00** Light and fragrant, with a candle wax edge to the raspberry and currant fruit. Ready now. ✪

85 HESS SELECT Cabernet Sauvignon California 1993 **$9.50** Ripe and compact, with attractive cherry and berry flavors that are well focused. This delivers a good bang for the buck, finishing with spicy, earthy notes. ✪

85 MCDOWELL Cabernet Sauvignon Mendocino 1992 **$10.00** Firm and chunky, with a decent core of currant, plum and cedary oak flavors that fold together nicely. Best after 1997.

85 TAFT STREET Cabernet Sauvignon California 1992 **$9.50** Supple and generous, a mouthful of currant and berry fruit that rolls on through the nicely polished finish. Ready now.

85 M.G. VALLEJO Cabernet Sauvignon California 1992 **$6.00** This is smooth and shines with bright fruit flavors, offering raspberry, strawberry, vanilla and a touch of herb on the supple finish. Approachable now, and at an attractive price. ✪

85 WENTE BROS. Cabernet Sauvignon Livermore Valley Wente Family Estate Selection 1993 **$8.00** A sturdy California wine that offers a lot for a fair price. The solid, beet-scented berry and herb flavors pick up interesting notes of spice and pickle barrel on the finish. ✪

84 BEL ARBORS Cabernet Sauvignon California 1993 **$7.00** Soft and generous, centered around appealing vanilla-scented raspberry and red currant flavors that linger gently on the finish. A fair price for a Cabernet of good quality. Drinkable now. ✪

84 CASTLEVIEW Cabernet Sauvignon Napa Valley Private Reserve 1993 **$9.00** Marked by herb and oaky flavors and modest plum and cherry notes, but the cedary oak flavors stand out.

84 CEDAR BROOK Cabernet Sauvignon Napa Valley 1993 **$7.00** Smooth and inviting, a lighter style that unfolds some appealing currant and anise flavors. Drinkable now.

84 CHRISTOPHE Cabernet Sauvignon Napa County 1992 **$9.00** Light, bright and simple, fragrant with berry and vanilla flavors. Approachable now.

84 ESTANCIA Cabernet Sauvignon Sonoma-Napa Counties 1993 **$10.00** Tight with an earthy, cedary edge to the wild berry and spice notes. Well balanced.

84 FETZER Cabernet Sauvignon California Bel Arbors 1993 **$7.00** Soft and generous, centered around appealing vanilla-scented raspberry and red currant flavors that linger gently on the finish. Approachable now.

84 GLASS MOUNTAIN QUARRY Cabernet Sauvignon California 1992 **$10.00** Light, refreshing and straightforward, offering berry and spice flavors that stay with you on the supple finish. Ready now. ✪

84 HAYWOOD Cabernet Sauvignon California Vintner's Select 1993 **$8.00** Smells funky, but the flavors pick up lovely raspberry accents, polished by spicy, toasty notes. Drinkable now. ✪

84 MILLSTREAM Cabernet Sauvignon California 1993 **$5.50** Smooth and exuberantly fruity, wheeling its raspberry, tobacco and spice flavors through the polished finish. Ready now.

84 REDWOOD CANYON Cabernet Sauvignon California 1993 **$8.00** Ripe and fruity, with supple plum and currant notes of modest proportion. Picks up a spicy edge on the finish.

84 SEGHESIO Cabernet Sauvignon Sonoma County Home Ranch 1993 **$9.50** Good intensity, with lively mint-, cherry- and plum-laced flavors before the tannins kick in. A solid value at this price.

84 MICHAEL SULLBERG Cabernet Sauvignon Central Coast 1992 **$6.00** Dry and intense, with a leathery oak edge to the currant- and berry-laced fruit. Finishes with a strong dose of sage and mint.

83 COTES DE SONOMA Cabernet Sauvignon Sonoma County 1993 **$8.00** Earthy, with mature color and flavors, dried fruit and a decadent edge. Spicy currant and cherry flavors hold it together.

83 CRESTON Cabernet Sauvignon Paso Robles 1992 **$10.00** Distinct for its wild berry and cherry fruit, but comes across as one dimensional, finishing with firm, dry oak and tannins.

83 GEYSER PEAK Cabernet Sauvignon Alexander Valley 1993 **$10.00** Clean and well balanced, with spicy berry and cherry flavors. Drink now. ✪

83 HAHN Cabernet Sauvignon Santa Lucia Highlands 1992 **$10.00** Austere, with firm tannins and a rustic, cedary edge to the Cabernet fruit, focusing on cherry and plum.

83 MONTEVINA Cabernet Sauvignon California 1992 **$9.00** Firm and chewy, a tight little wine that manages to sneak in some lovely berry flavor on the finish. Try in 1998.

83 NOMINEE Cabernet Sauvignon Paso Robles 1993 **$7.00** Firm and tight, with a well balanced band of currant, cedar and spice.

83 RIVER ROAD Cabernet Sauvignon Napa County 1993 **$9.00** Light, smooth and appealing, its berry and currant flavors are nicely integrated.

83 ROUND HILL Cabernet Sauvignon California 1992 **$7.00** Soft and generous, a simple wine with strawberry and light plum fruit that hangs in there on the finish. Ready now. ✪

83 RUSTY STAUB'S Cabernet Sauvignon California 1992 **$10.00** A fruity style with wild berry and raspberry notes, turning smooth and polished on the finish. Simple and pleasing.

83 STEVENOT Cabernet Sauvignon Sierra Foothills 1993 **$7.00** Strikes a nice balance between smoky, toasty oak and ripe, spicy berry flavor.

83 WOODBRIDGE Cabernet Sauvignon California Barrel Aged 1992 **$6.50** Simple but pleasant, with ripe cherry and strawberry jam notes, picking up a spicy edge. ✪

82 ARCIERO Cabernet Sauvignon Paso Robles 1992 **$9.00** Light and silky behind the chewy tannins, showing appealing raspberry and toasty flavors on a modest scale. Best after 1998-1999.

82 DUNNEWOOD Cabernet Sauvignon Alexander Valley Seven Arches Vineyard Gold Label Select 1992 **$10.00** Marked by green olive and herb flavors with a touch of dill and bell pepper flavors that override the cherry and plum notes. Finishes with firm tannins.

82 FETZER Cabernet Sauvignon California Valley Oaks 1993 **$8.00** Light, straightforward, showing nice plum and berry flavors that fade a bit on the finish. Ready now.

82 GLEN ELLEN Cabernet Sauvignon California Proprietor's Reserve 1993 **$6.00** Light, focused around raspberry and a touch of mint; smooth and drinkable now.

82 J. LOHR Cabernet Sauvignon California Cypress 1993 **$8.00** Bright, fruity and simple, generous with its berry flavors, finishing soft. ○

82 LOUIS M. MARTINI Cabernet Sauvignon North Coast 1992 **$9.50** Light and modestly fragrant, a simple wine with berry and spice notes. Drink now. ○

82 MOONDANCE Cabernet Sauvignon Napa Valley 1992 **$10.00** Marked by cedary tobacco and earthy nuances, just enough herb and currant flavors coming through to maintain balance. Best in 1997, but may always be tannic.

82 MOUNT KONOCTI Cabernet Sauvignon Lake County 1993 **$10.00** A bit rustic, with chewy tannins and earthy wild berry flavors.

82 R.H. PHILLIPS Cabernet Sauvignon California 1992 **$7.00** Medium-bodied with a cedary accent on the ripe plum and cherry flavors. Offers modest depth. ✪

82 PLAM Cabernet Sauvignon California 1992 **$6.00** Smooth and polished, with earthy herb, cherry and a spicy pickley edge, finishing with fine tannins. Ready. ✪

82 STEVENOT Cabernet Sauvignon Calveras County Reserve 1992 **$10.00** Manages to balance its ripe berry and cherry flavors against the earthy, somewhat rubbery notes.

81 ROBERT ALISON Cabernet Sauvignon California 1993 **$6.00** A strong tobacco flavor runs through the light currant flavors in this soft-textured red.

81 MONTHAVEN Cabernet Sauvignon Napa Valley 1993 **$8.00** Pleasant enough, with ripe cherry, currant and berry flavors of modest proportion.

81 STRATFORD Cabernet Sauvignon Napa Valley 1993 **$10.00** A lean wine with flavors that run toward pickle barrel and toast, modest on the fruit. Tannic enough to want until 1998 or even 2000.

80 C K MONDAVI Cabernet Sauvignon California 1993 **$6.50** Light and gently fruity, hinting at plum and currant on the modest finish.

80 IVAN TAMAS Cabernet Sauvignon Livermore Valley 1992 **$7.00** Light in texture, vegetal with berry and beet flavors swinging through. Drinkable now.

WASHINGTON

89 PRESTON WINE CELLARS Cabernet Sauvignon Washington Oak Aged 1993 **$10.00** Smooth, ripe and generous, opening up to a cascade of berry, plum, spice and vanilla flavors that swirl around elegantly on the finish. Approachable now.

87 COLUMBIA CREST Cabernet Sauvignon Columbia Valley 1993 **$9.00** Dense and chewy without being rough, packed with ripe cherry and spice flavors that turn toward elegance on the finish. Delicious now. ✪

87 STE. CHAPELLE Cabernet Sauvignon Washington 1993 **$10.00** Firm in texture, with brightly focused grapy berry flavors that remain lively on the finish. Drinkable now.

86 WASHINGTON HILLS Cabernet Sauvignon Columbia Valley Varietal Select 1993 **$9.00** Lean and chewy, flirting with oak up front, but ripe fruit comes bouncing back on the tannic finish, echoing currant and plum.

84 PAUL THOMAS Cabernet Sauvignon Washington 1994 **$9.50** A little light and lean, but showing enough freshness on the finish to make it approachable.

82 MARBLE CREST Cabernet Sauvignon Columbia Valley 1993 **$8.00** Soft and generous, centered around gentle plum and berry flavors. Ready now.

Merlot

CALIFORNIA

89 BLACKSTONE Merlot Napa County Reserve 1993 **$10.00** Serves up ripe, polished cherry, currant and light, smoky oak shadings. A red of finesse and grace; hard to beat at this price.

88 PARDUCCI Merlot California 1994 **$8.00** Smooth and polished, with pretty coffee, toasty oak and wild berry flavors that pick up nice, spicy notes on the finish. Hard to find a better value in Merlot anywhere. ✪

86 J. LOHR Merlot California Cypress 1993 **$10.00** Strives for complexity with its toasty, smoky oak, but comes across as a bit disjointed. Short-term cellaring should help. ✪

86 MONTERRA Merlot Monterey Sand Hill 1992 **$10.00** Elegant and fruity, adding just a trace of herb. Bright cherry and berry flavors are well defined. Medium-bodied, mild tannins. Drinks well now.

86 TESSERA Merlot California 1994 **$9.00** A crisp, well-focused and mildly tannic wine packed with bright berry and anise flavors.

85 FETZER Merlot California Eagle Peak 1994 **$8.00** The flavors edge strongly toward black cherry and a hint of chocolate on a light, open-textured frame. A bit tannic, should be fine with hearty food. At this price, it's a good off-the-shelf red. ✪

85 CHATEAU JULIEN Merlot Monterey County Grand Reserve 1994 **$9.00** Light and appealing, with ripe currant and blueberry flavors and a smooth finish. Drinkable now.

85 NAPA RIDGE Merlot North Coast Coastal 1993 **$10.00** Smooth and flavorful, with tasty black cherry, spice and herbal flavors that linger delicately on the finish.

84 BEL ARBOR Merlot California Vintner's Selection 1994 **$6.00** Light, smooth and refreshing, with raspberry and spice flavors that linger gently on the finish. ✪

84 CANYON ROAD Merlot California 1993 **$8.00** Lacks focus, but the currant, herb and tea notes are complex enough, and certainly a bargain at this level. Better than many Merlots at twice its price.

83 LOUIS M. MARTINI Merlot North Coast 1994 **$9.50** Light, bright and lively, with modest strawberry flavors and a hint of mint on the finsh. ✪

83 MONTPELLIER Merlot California 1993 **$8.00** Openly fruity, with ripe, juicy cherry, plum and berry notes that are medium bodied. Simple but pleasant.

82 HAHN Merlot Santa Lucia Highlands 1993 **$10.00** A vegetal streak adds flashes of bell pepper, but it gathers enough plum and cherry flavor to create interest. ✪

82 TALUS Merlot California 1994 **$8.00** Light and peppery, with a blueberry edge to the earthy flavors. ✪

81 SILVER RIDGE Merlot California Barrel Select 1992 **$10.00** Medium-bodied, with simple cherry and berry fruit flavors and light oak shadings with mild tannins. Good but nothing more.

80 CANYON ROAD Merlot California 1994 **$7.00** Light in texture, with plummy, spicy notes that never quite come into focus.

80 ROUND HILL Merlot California 1993 **$8.00** Simple and rustic, with cedary, cherry flavors that are dry at the start and become even dryer on the finish.

WASHINGTON

88 COLUMBIA CREST Merlot Columbia Valley 1993 **$10.00** Ripe, smooth and distinctly gamy, making this a Washington red that gives you some character for the money. There's a hint of the barnyard in the delicious blackberry and currant flavors. Fine tannins will hold this through 1998. ✪

85 WASHINGTON HILLS Merlot Columbia Valley Varietal Select 1993 **$9.00** Broad and supple, concentrating its plum, currant and tar flavors in a slightly chewy package.

84 STONE CREEK Merlot Washington Special Selection 1993 **$8.00** A distinctly floral character spices up this light-textured, flavorful red that echoes spice and berry. Has enough tannin to flourish through 1998. A good price for all that. ✪

83 PRESTON WINE CELLARS Merlot Washington Oak Aged 1993 **$10.00** Rich and full-bodied, a strong herbal, earthy streak cutting through the chunky black cherry flavors. May be best in 1998.

81 WORDEN Merlot Washington 1993 **$8.00** Light, lean and spicy raspberry and watermelon flavors dance across the finish. Ready now.

80 MARBLE CREST Merlot Columbia Valley 1993 **$10.00** A lean and spicy, pickle-barrel character overtakes the fruit.

Pinot Noir

CALIFORNIA

87 PARDUCCI Pinot Noir Mendocino County 1994 **$8.00** Complex and well oaked for this price category, with a strong toasty oak and vanilla edge to the ripe cherry and wild berry flavors.

86 ARIES Pinot Noir Los Carneros 1994 **$10.00** Marked by spicy, toasty oak and a supple core of cherry and wild berry flavor. Very appealing, ready-to-drink-now style.

86 BUENA VISTA Pinot Noir Carneros 1993 **$10.00** Light and appealing for its lively vanilla-scented berry flavors that linger on the finish. Another winner from this value-oriented California winery.

86 NAPA RIDGE Pinot Noir North Coast Coastal 1994 **$7.50** Smooth and polished, with a pretty core of cherry and plum and a toasty oak overlay. Attractive for its value. ✪

85 CARNEROS CREEK Pinot Noir Carneros Fleur de Carneros 1994 **$10.00** Tight and tannic, yet styled for early drinking. The wild berry and cherry flavors come through, and it's a bargain for a California Pinot. ✪

85 CEDAR BROOK Pinot Noir California 1993 **$7.00** Light in texture, but it has a Port-like, smoky, ripe edge to the flavors, making it intriguing through the spicy finish. Drinkable now.

85 LOUIS M. MARTINI Pinot Noir Los Carneros 1993 **$8.00** A touch earthy, with dried cherry and plum flavors, finishing with a pleasant mushroom edge. Very appealing, and a wonderful buy at this price. Has 14 percent Petite Sirah, which pushes the tannins a bit.

84 BRINDIAMO Pinot Noir Edna Valley Limited Bottling 1993 **$10.00** Firm and tannic, medium in weight, showing pleasant cherry, berry and cola notes.

84 ESTANCIA Pinot Noir Monterey 1994 **$10.00** Pleasantly fruity in an uncomplicated way, supple, offering plum and cherry notes of modest proportion.

83 CHATEAU DE BAUN Pinot Noir Russian River Valley 1992 **$10.00** Very light, with raspberry flavors and earthy, animal notes that linger gently on the finish.

83 PEPPERWOOD GROVE Pinot Noir California Cask Lot One 1993 **$6.00** Light and plummy, keeping its fruit singing on the light finish. Has style.

83 SONOMA CREEK Pinot Noir Sonoma County 1993 **$10.00** A lighter style with herb, tea and spice notes, finishing with a light black cherry edge.

82 BEAULIEU Pinot Noir California Beautour 1994 **$10.00** Light and fruity, with an appealing core of cherry and berry fruit of modest proportion.

82 BOUCHAINE Pinot Noir California Q.C. Fly 1993 **$8.50** Light and smooth, with nice toast and cherry flavors running through it.

82 CRESTON Pinot Noir Paso Robles 1994 **$10.00** Light, with modest wild berry and cherry flavors. A wine to drink now.

82 CHATEAU DE BAUN Pinot Noir Russian River Valley 1993 **$10.00** Light and uncomplicated, marked by toasty oak and a narrow band of dried cherry flavor underneath.

82 VILLA MT. EDEN Pinot Noir California Cellar Select 1994 **$8.00** Offers a modest core of plum and cherry flavors, but you won't feel shortchanged at this price. Drinkable now.

81 CHARLES KRUG Pinot Noir Carneros Napa Valley 1993 **$9.00** Light and simple, with cherry-berry flavors of modest depth and proportion.

81 NAVARRO Pinot Noir Anderson Valley Table Wine 1993 **$10.00** Simple but pleasant with cherry and berry flavors of modest proportion. Ready now, might even work well slightly chilled.

80 MIRASSOU Pinot Noir Monterey County
Fifth Generation Family Selection 1992 **$7.00**
Light, straightforward, modest in flavor, offering some
nice plum and toast flavors.

80 M.G. VALLEJO Pinot Noir California Harvest
Select 1994 **$8.00** Light and simple, with modest fruit
flavors that may possibly remind you of Pinot Noir.

80 CHRISTINE WOODS Pinot Noir Anderson
Valley NV **$10.00** Old style California Pinot, show-
ing firm tannins and earthy cherry and berry notes,
turning crisp and a bit leathery on the finish.

Oregon

87 DOMAIN HILL & MAYES Pinot Noir Oregon
Van Duzer Appellation Selection 1992 **$10.00** A
big, powerful style that emphasizes ripe flavors and
smoky, toasty grace notes over brightness and elegance.
A good value for all that.

87 TUALATIN Pinot Noir Willamette Valley
Barrel Aged 1994 **$10.00** Lithe and racy, zingy with
raspberry and blackberry flavors that linger through
the bright finish. A terrific buy for a Pinot whose fine
tannins are ready now.

86 FIRESTEED Pinot Noir Oregon 1994 **$10.00**
Lithe and silky, generous with its leafy plum and
berry flavors, yet easy on the wallet. Fine tannins.

85 AURORA Pinot Noir Willamette Valley 1993 **$9.00** Soft, almost delicate, sporting marvelous plum and berry flavors hovering around the finish. Drink now.

85 BETHEL HEIGHTS Pinot Noir Willamette Valley First Release 1994 **$10.00** Bright and flavorful, racy wild berry flavors loping through the finish. Drinkable now.

84 HENRY Pinot Noir Oregon Umpqua Cuvée 1994 **$9.00** An open style of wine, fragrant, simple and generous with its berry flavors. Ready now.

83 BRIDGEVIEW Pinot Noir Oregon Reserve 1993 **$10.00** Smooth and refined, velvety, fine tannins, offering plummy, spicy flavors that narrow on the finish. Approachable now.

83 ELKTON VALLEY Pinot Noir Umpqua Valley 1994 **$9.00** Smooth and nicely balanced, playing its black cherry and spice flavors against a light texture on the finish. Ready now.

83 HINMAN VINEYARDS Pinot Noir Oregon 1994 **$10.00** Firm and chewy with fine tannins and showing a modest level of prune and berry flavors. Drinkable now.

82 MONTINORE Pinot Noir Willamette Valley 1993 **$10.00** Soft and appealing, light in color, and has a spicy edge to the raisiny black cherry flavors. Drinkable now.

81 DUCK POND Pinot Noir Willamette Valley 1993 **$8.00** Light in texture but ripe in flavor, modest in intensity, with some nice earthy cherry flavors on the finish. Drinkable now.

80 AIRLIE Pinot Noir Willamette Valley 1993 **$10.00** Lean, floral and distinctly herbal. This is fine-textured, but it needs some richness or ripeness to balance out. Try in 1997.

80 BRIDGEVIEW Pinot Noir Oregon 1994 **$6.00** Light and surprisingly tannic; this is tight, with simple berry flavors. Drinkable now.

Syrah

CALIFORNIA

88 R.H. PHILLIPS Syrah California EXP 1993 **$10.00** Smooth and polished, with a core of supple cherry and berry flavors. Firms up on the finish where the tannins become more evident. Try now.

87 MCDOWELL Syrah Mendocino 1993 **$10.00** Ripe and generous, focusing its plum and berry flavors nicely against the velvety background. Good value for a California Syrah with this much character. Drink now.

82 SOBON ESTATE Syrah Shenandoah Valley 1993 **$10.00** Earthy, gamy flavors dominate this gutsy, chewy red. Has a little black cherry note on the finish.

81 REY SOL Syrah Temecula 1994 **$10.00** Earthy, musty notes divert the focus of the modest pepper and berry flavors. More characteristic of a red table wine than a Syrah.

Zinfandel

CALIFORNIA

89 VIANO Zinfandel Contra Costa County Sand Rock Hill Reserve Selection 1992 **$9.00** Intense and spicy, packed with well-focused black cherry, currant and plum notes. Turns firmly tannic on the finish, where it picks up a toasty oak flavor. Well balanced.

88 VILLA MT. EDEN Zinfandel California Cellar Select 1993 **$8.00** Pleasantly balanced, with a nice mix of currant, black cherry and wild berry flavors. Firm tannins and a touch of oak are part of the appeal. Great value, and drinkable now through 1997.

87 BERINGER Zinfandel Napa Valley 1992 **$9.00** Strikes a nice balance between the ripe and supple cherry and raspberry flavors and the spicy anise notes. Manages to pull off a smooth and supple style, even with its tannins showing. Good value for this kind of complexity. ✪

87 KARLY Zinfandel Amador County Pokerville 1993 **$8.00** A touch earthy, but the cherry and wild berry flavors are very ripe and floral in this bargain of a California red. Hints of jam seep in around the palate and the fruity finish shows dry tannins.

87 PEIRANO ESTATE Zinfandel Lodi 1993 **$10.00** Dense and plush, with a firm, tannic aspect to the cherry and plum flavors. Well crafted. Drinks well now.

87 SHENANDOAH Zinfandel Amador County Special Reserve 1994 **$8.50** Young and still some-what raw and tannic but well balanced, featuring a pleasant core of smoky, toasty, berry flavors. Finishes on the short side; aging into 1997 is advised.

87 CHATEAU SOUVERAIN Zinfandel Dry Creek Valley 1993 **$9.50** Smooth and well integrated, with modest cherry, spice and wild berry flavors that finish off with soft tannins and a touch of oak. Nice sub-tleties in a California red of this price range.

87 WHITE OAK Zinfandel Sonoma Valley 1993 **$9.00** A well-built Zin, with a chunky core of cherry and menthol flavors, finishing with a firmly tannic edge. Try now.

86 BYINGTON Zinfandel Howell Mountain 1992 **$10.00** Ripe and appealing for its wild berry and plum-laced flavors, picking up a hint of prune on the finish. Tannins are in the right proportion.

85 ACACIA Zinfandel Napa Valley Old Vines 1993 **$10.00** Appealingly ripe, supple and complex with its berry, cherry, spice and light oak shadings. Well mannered and the tannins are soft.

85 BERINGER Zinfandel North Coast 1992 **$10.00** Well-balanced, bright berry and cherry flavors, hints of spice, fine tannins and clean finish. Drinkable now. ○

85 MILANO Zinfandel Mendocino County Sanel Valley Vineyard 1993 **$10.00** Intense and well-focused cherry, wild berry and raspberry notes are ripe, elegant and supple.

85 ROUND HILL Zinfandel Napa Valley 1992 **$8.00** Intense and lively, with spicy, minty aromatics and attractive wild berry and cherry flavors. Well crafted.

85 RUTHERFORD RANCH Zinfandel Napa Valley 1992 **$8.00** Ripe and jammy, showing hints of raisin and tar, which give this some unique flavors. Turns spicy and elegant on the finish, and reveals a touch of heat.

85 SEGHESIO Zinfandel Sonoma County 1993 **$9.00** Tight, firm and tannic, with a narrow band of earthy berry and cherry. Tannins clamp down on the finish, but enough fruit sneaks past to hold your interest. Can age a little. ○

84 BUEHLER Zinfandel Napa Valley 1993
$10.00 Ripe and earthy, the intense cherry, leather, oak and anise flavors folding together nicely. Better than a previous bottle tasted.

84 CASTORO Zinfandel Paso Robles 1992
$10.00 Mature, earthy and cedary, but it holds together, turning fruitier on the finish where the cherry and berry notes fill it out.

84 KALINDA Zinfandel Paso Robles 1991 **$9.00**
Appealing for its supple raspberry and cherry notes, this also adds a nicely spicy twist on the finish.

84 LOLONIS Zinfandel Mendocino County 1992
$10.00 A touch meaty, but the wild berry and cherry flavors come through in this lean and crisp wine. It's not the Private Reserve, but a good value.

84 MADRONA Zinfandel El Dorado 1992 **$8.50**
Medium-bodied and smooth, with cherry and berry flavors that are simple but pleasing.

84 MARTIN BROTHERS Zinfandel Paso Robles La Primitiva 1993 **$10.00** Tight and compact, with a narrow band of spicy berry and cherry flavors and firm tannins.

84 RABBIT RIDGE Zinfandel Sonoma County 1994 **$10.00** Ripe and spicy, with pretty plum, cherry and berry jam notes of modest proportion. Drinks well now.

84 SAUSAL Zinfandel Alexander Valley 1994
$10.00 A solid value, featuring earthy berry and
spice flavors and adding firm tannins and good intensity on the finish.

84 TELDESCHI Zinfandel Sonoma County 1990
$10.00 Showing its mature flavors, with an earthy,
cedary character to the berry and spice notes.
Drink now.

83 AMADOR FOOTHILL Zinfandel Shenandoah
Valley Ferrero Vineyard 1991 **$10.00** Crisp but
earthy; the cherry, raspberry are lightly shaded by
oak, though it's showing more mature flavors at this
stage than expected.

83 ANGELINE Zinfandel California Old Vine
Cuvée 1992 **$8.00** Notes of earth, tar and berry
accompany chewy tannins, finishing leathery. Has
lots of flavor but rustic.

83 ARCIERO Zinfandel Paso Robles 1992
$7.50 Has intense, jammy aromas, but not too rich on
the palate, where pleasant, earthy wild berry flavors
dominate.

83 BOGLE Zinfandel California 1993 **$6.00**
Well-oaked so the toasty wood flavors stand out, but
the wild berry, cherry and blueberry flavors keep it
interesting.

83 FORESTVILLE Zinfandel California 1993
$5.50 Simple, earthy cherry and wild berry notes
pick up a jammy edge on the finish.

83 FREY Zinfandel Mendocino 1993 **$8.00** Stays in bounds while stretching the limits, with medium-weight black cherry, spice and light tannins.

83 HIDDEN CELLARS Zinfandel Mendocino McAdams Vineyard 1993 **$10.00** Modest but balanced, with appealing berry and cherry notes. Tasted twice, with consistent notes.

83 MADRONA Zinfandel El Dorado 1993 **$9.00** Clean and pleasant enough but nothing special, adding hints of spice, pepper and wild berry. Firmly tannic.

83 MIRASSOU Zinfandel Central Coast Fifth Generation Family Selection 1992 **$7.00** On the lighter side, both in color and body, but has appealing cherry and berry notes of modest proportions.

83 MONTEVINA Zinfandel Amador County 1993 **$7.00** Rustic and shows a meaty side to the tannic wild berry flavors. Starts to grow on you, though, by the second or third sip.

83 MONTEVINA Zinfandel Amador County Brioso 1994 **$6.50** A lighter style marked by fresh berry and strawberry flavors. Might work well served slightly chilled. Drinkable now.

83 MONTPELLIER Zinfandel California 1993 **$7.00** Strikes a pleasant balance between the ripe cherry, plum and wild berry flavors and the modest tannins.

83 PEACHY CANYON Zinfandel Paso Robles Incredible Red Bin 102 NV **$9.50** Light and fruity, with simple but pleasant cherry and berry flavors. Drinkable now.

83 PEPPERWOOD GROVE Zinfandel California 1993 **$6.00** Correct and well proportioned. Has wild berry, cherry and strawberry notes. Good price, too.

83 ROSENBLUM Zinfandel California Vintners Cuvee X NV **$8.00** Earthy but shows hints of wild berry and spice. A solid Zin for everyday drinking.

83 ROUND HILL Zinfandel Napa Valley 1993 **$10.00** Firm and tannic, with strong tar and anise flavors. There is just enough spicy cherry and berry to keep your attention. Good, but off-pace for this winery, which usually does better.

83 STONE CREEK Zinfandel California Special Selection 1991 **$7.00** Mature and earthy, with notes of berry and tar. Finishes crisply acidic, with firm tannins.

83 STORY Zinfandel Shenandoah Valley 1992 **$10.00** The earthy, tarry character dominates the simple cherry and berry notes, but the flavors grow on you. Will show better with food.

83 YORK MOUNTAIN Zinfandel San Luis Obispo County 1991 **$9.00** Ultraripe, jammy and prunelike, but also bearing a subtle pungency. A full-blown style that picks up a tart, earthy, slightly hot aftertaste.

82 E. & J. GALLO Zinfandel North Coast 1992 **$6.00** A touch leathery, but enough wild berry and cherry flavors hang in there to keep it in balance. ✪

82 KARLY Zinfandel Amador County 1993 **$10.00** An earthy, gamy style that is slightly funky, but it holds together. Enough wild berry flavors keep your interest.

82 TALUS Zinfandel California 1993 **$7.00** Solid if rustic, with chunky wild berry and cherry flavors that turn crisp and a touch stemmy on the finish.

82 WOODBRIDGE Zinfandel California Barrel Aged 1993 **$5.00** A touch earthy, with a green-tealike edge, but the wild berry and cherry flavors rise up and make it palatable. ✪

81 SOBON ESTATE Zinfandel Shenandoah Valley 1992 **$10.00** A rustic style, with cherry and berry jam flavors and a tarry character. Tannic and earthy on the finish.

80 RADANOVICH Zinfandel Sierra Foothills 1993 **$9.50** Pleasant enough, offering a tarry plum edge and mild tannins. Drinkable now.

80 STEVENOT Zinfandel Sierra Foothills Reserve 1993 **$8.00** Light but has some simple spice, berry and oaky notes that are pleasant.

Other Red Varietals

87 BONNY DOON Grenache California Clos de Gilroy 1994 **$8.00** Medium weight, with pretty, supple plum and cherry notes that linger on the finish, turning a bit grapey.

87 NOCETO Sangiovese Shenandoah Valley 1994 **$10.00** Ripe and attractive layers of currant and black cherry flavors, with spice and anise notes. Well balanced, nicely focused and flavorful on the finish.

86 BOGLE Petite Sirah California 1993 **$7.00** Smooth and remarkably polished, a solid red with appealing berry, spice and vanilla flavors that roll languidly across the palate. Approachable now with food, best from 1997.

86 PARDUCCI Petite Sirah Mendocino County 1992 **$6.50** Smooth and concentrated, with plum and bright strawberry flavors that weave neatly through the vanilla-scented finish. Offers elegance and value.

86 PRESTON Gamay Beaujolais Dry Creek Valley 1995 **$9.00** Youthful, ripe and disarmingly delicious, sporting bright berry and dusky spice flavors. Drink it soon.

85 SHOOTING STAR Grenache Washington Côte de Columbia 1994 **$8.50** Smooth, fruity and generous with its blackberry, plum and spice flavors. From a California winery, but with Washington grapes.

84 BONNY DOON Grenache American Clos de Gilroy Cuvée St. Marcel NV **$8.50** Snappy, crushed pepper, cherry and wild berry flavors in a fresh and lively, nouveau style.

84 MARTIN BROTHERS Nebbiolo Central Coast 1993 **$10.00** Fruity, light, showing nice raspberry and vanilla flavors that echo on the supple finish. Ready now.

84 MONTEVINA Barbera Amador County 1993 **$9.00** An elegant, medium-weight style, showing bright, tart cherry and berry flavors.

83 BONNY DOON Cabernet Franc California Pacific Rim 1994 **$10.00** Young and still showing fermentation aromas, but the fruit is ripe and pure, with currant and cherry notes, lacking extra dimensions but pleasant enough.

83 OBESTER Sangiovese Mendocino County 1993 **$10.00** Soft in texture and bright, showing modest strawberry flavor and a mildly grapey character. Drinkable now.

83 STRATFORD Dolcetto Napa Valley 1994 **$8.50** Lightly floral, fruity and simple, an easy wine to drink as an apéritif or with light lunch.

82 BONNY DOON Charbono California Ca' del Solo La Farfalla 1994 **$10.00** Smells floral and fruity, but is tight and compact on the palate with hints of cherry and berry flavors.

82 BONNY DOON Grenache California Clos de Gilroy 1994 **$8.00** A wine marked by soft, banana and berry fruit, with good concentration. An easy-drinking summer quaffer.

82 FOPPIANO Petite Sirah Sonoma County 1992 **$9.50** Chewy and tannic at first, but the solid plum and berry flavors come through as the tannins become more polished on the finish. Best from 1997.

82 MONTE VOLPE Barbera California 1992 **$9.00** Simple, earthy and a little tart, with modest beet and berry flavors sneaking in on the finish. Maybe best from 1997.

81 BERINGER Gamay Beaujolais California Nouveau 1995 **$7.50** Very light, striving for delicacy in color and flavor and showing a modicum of pleasant berry notes.

81 MONTHAVEN Malbec Napa Valley 1993 **$8.00** Austere and stalky, the unripe character of the modest plum and currant flavors barely holding your interest.

81 PELLEGRINI FAMILY Barbera Sonoma Valley Old Vines 1993 **$10.00** Light, watery berry, earth and spice notes.

Other Reds

87 LAUREL GLEN Red California 1993 **$7.00** A firm and tight value wine that has some herbal tones in its wild berry and plum aromas and flavors. Finishes firmly tannic.

85 KIONA LEMBERGER YAKIMA VALLEY 1993
$10.00 Light and vibrant blackberry and spice fla-
vors, appealing to drink right now.

85 MONTEVINA Montanaro Amador County
1992 **$7.50** Light in texture and a little chewy with
tannins, but the plum and black cherry flavors hold
their own on the finish. Drink now with hearty food,
or age until 1998.

82 HOGUE LEMBERGER YAKIMA VALLEY
1993 **$9.00** Fruity, sturdy and simple, showing a nice
touch of blackberry flavor. Ready now.

85 TOBIN JAMES Chateau Le Cacheflo Central
Coast NV **$7.00** Light-textured but snappy in flavor,
delivering a nice mouthful of wild berry, raspberry
and plum that lingers on the lively finish. Ready now.

84 MONTEVINA Matrimonio Amador County
1992 **$8.50** Crisp in texture, with a nice thread of
smooth black currant and berry flavors that bring
some suppleness to the finish.

81 JADE MOUNTAIN Cotes Du Soleil California
Red 1994 **$8.00** Has dusty, meaty flavors and ripe
cherry too, but it's coarse and tannic on the finish.

80 R.H. PHILLIPS Alliance Red California 1992
$9.00 Rustic, rough-and-tumble style that relies too
much on high-extract tannins. Cherry, berry and waxy
flavors are submerged underneath and really don't
shine through. Slightly bitter finish. Mourvèdre and
Syrah.

80 R.H. PHILLIPS Mistura Night Harvest Dunnigan Hills 1994 **$6.00** Simple, modest fruit flavors that develop a dry, clay-like edge when mixed with the tannins.

80 WHITE HERON Chantepierre Washington 1992 **$10.00** Lean and a bit tannic, herbal notes mingling with the modest plum and spicy prune flavors. Drink now.

WHITE

Chardonnay

CALIFORNIA

89 MERIDIAN Chardonnay Santa Barbara County 1994 **$10.00** Brimming with fresh, ripe pear, apricot, peach and spicy fruit flavors, a rich and forward style that leads into a pretty, creamy, fruity aftertaste. Hard to beat at this price—or even twice this price. ✪

88 BELVEDERE Chardonnay Sonoma County 1994 **$9.00** Ripe, bright, vivid pear, peach and nectarine notes pick up a trace of oak and hazelnut on the lingering finish. A well-crafted white that delivers a load of flavors. ✪

88 EXPRESSIONS Chardonnay Sonoma County 1994 **$10.00** Harmonious and focused, letting its peach, pear and vanilla flavors emerge gently on the round finish. A great value that's drinkable now. From Glen Ellen. ✪

87 ABADIA DEL ROBLE Chardonnay California Barrel Fermented 1994 **$10.00** Ripe with honey, peach, pear and spice notes, but also a good dose of oak, which gives it a dry, woody edge on the finish.

87 BELVEDERE Chardonnay Alexander Valley 1993 **$10.00** There's plenty of oak here, lending toasty, buttery flavors, but it also has enough rich pear and apple notes to keep it in balance. A value of a California Chardonnay.

87 CARNEROS CREEK Chardonnay California Fleur de Carneros 1993 **$9.00** Clean and fruity, with ripe pear, honey and apple notes that develop depth and complexity on the finish. It offers much for this price.

87 DREYER SONOMA Chardonnay Sonoma County 1994 **$9.00** Fresh and floral, a Chardonnay of modest scale but charming for its spicy pear flavors. Ready now.

87 HESS SELECT Chardonnay California 1994 **$9.50** Fresh and flavorful, with apricot and pear flavors swirling refreshingly through it. Drinkable now. ✪

87 PARDUCCI Chardonnay Mendocino County 1994 **$8.00** Smooth, fruity and distinctly spicy, weaving a nutmeg-cinnamon character through its pear and smoke flavors. It's a good value to boot. ✪

87 R.H. PHILLIPS Chardonnay Dunnigan Hills Barrel Cuvée 1994 **$8.00** Light, elegant and surprisingly deep in flavor, which makes this low-priced California white quite notable. This adds extra facets of spice and hazelnut to the pear and apricot flavors. ✪

87 WILSON DANIELS Chardonnay Napa Valley 1993 **$10.00** Bright and focused, showing a distinct toasty, spicy streak through the supple pear flavors. Drinkable now.

86 BANDIERA Chardonnay Napa Valley 1994 **$8.00** Bright and flavorful, with lively apple and citrus flavors tempered by a touch of sweet vanilla. Good subtlety makes this a value. ✪

86 COTES DE SONOMA Chardonnay Sonoma County 1994 **$8.00** Lean and crisp, showing plenty of floral, citrus and apple flavors that remain vibrant on the finish. A Chardonnay that still delivers some charm without charging a premium.

86 FETZER Chardonnay North Coast Barrel Select 1994 **$10.00** Smooth in texture, with spicy apple and pear flavors in balance and echoing nicely on the finish.

86 HIDDEN CELLARS Chardonnay Mendocino Organically Grown Grapes 1993 **$10.00** Smooth, round and spicy, focusing its pear, nutmeg and caramel flavors through a tight finish. Drinkable now.

86 JOLIESSE VINEYARDS Chardonnay California Reserve 1994 **$7.00** Zingy, fruity and a bargain too. This offers a real mouthful of complex peach, pear and spice flavors. ✪

86 NEWLAN Chardonnay Napa Valley Napa-Villages 1992 **$10.00** Smooth and spicy, a streak of honey running through the silky pear and spice flavors which linger on the finish. Ready now.

86 SILVER RIDGE Chardonnay California Barrel Fermented 1994 **$10.00** Ripe and spicy, with generous nutmeg, toast and pear flavors that narrow to a sharp focus on the finish.

86 MICHAEL SULLBERG Chardonnay Knights Valley Lot 54 Barrel Fermented 1994 **$8.00** Light in texture but bright, featuring pear and vanilla flavors that finish with some restraint. Ready now.

86 TAFT STREET Chardonnay Sonoma County 1994 **$10.00** Soft and charming, offering up a nice mouthful of lightly spicy melon and pear flavors. This is a value white for drinking now.

85 BEL ARBORS Chardonnay California Vintner's Selection 1994 **$5.00** Fresh and appealing for its scent of lime and the pineapple and pear flavors, which echo nicely on the finish. Offers some excitement, and a steal at this price. ✪

85 FOREST GLEN Chardonnay California Barrel Fermented 1994 **$10.00** Distinctive for its core of butterscotch flavors, it also has a nice band of pear and spice, at a very attractive price. ✪

85 GLEN ELLEN Chardonnay California Proprietor's Reserve 1993 **$5.00** Features ripe, lively pineapple and grapefruit flavors that hang with you. Well made and a great value.

85 HAYWOOD Chardonnay California Vintner's Select 1994 **$8.00** Soft and broad in texture, centered around citrusy pear and toasty earthy flavors that spread on the finish. Ready now. ✪

85 J. LOHR Chardonnay California Cypress 1993 **$9.00** Light and fragrant, smooth-textured, showing plenty of spicy, leesy pear and apple flavor and a lingering finish. Drink now. ✪

85 LOUIS M. MARTINI Chardonnay Napa Valley 1994 **$9.00** Ripe and generous, floral around the edge of the orange, vanilla and pear flavors. Ready now. ✪

85 NAPA RIDGE Chardonnay Central Coast Coastal Vines 1994 **$7.50** Soft, creamy and disarmingly tasty, showing spicy orange and pear flavors that glide smoothly through the supple finish.

85 NAVARRO Chardonnay Mendocino 1994 **$8.00** Ripe and spicy, with a juicy core of citrus, pear and spice. Drinks well now.

85 CHATEAU POTELLE Chardonnay Napa Valley-Central Coast 1994 **$9.50** Intense and earthy with pronounced grassy overtones, straying into Sauvignon Blanc territory where it takes a citrus and grapefruit edge.

85 SILVERADO HILL CELLARS Chardonnay Napa Valley 1994 **$10.00** A light style that's harmonious and delicately spicy, accenting the green apple flavor.

85 WENTE BROS. Chardonnay Arroyo Seco Riva Ranch 1993 **$8.00** Smooth and satiny, wrapping its light pineapple and pear notes around a core of spicy, toasty flavors. Finishes in a flourish. Ready now.

85 WILDHURST Chardonnay California 1993 **$10.00** Crisp and spicy; ripe apple, pear, honey and vanilla notes turn complex and elegant on the finish, where oak folds in nicely. Very well made. ✪

84 LAWRENCE J. BARGETTO Chardonnay Central Coast Cypress 1994 **$9.00** Floral and perfumed, with a pleasant core of pear and citrus flavors. Medium-bodied, soft and ready.

84 BOUCHAINE Chardonnay California Q.C. Fly 1993 **$8.50** Lingering floral and pear flavors characterize this crisp, spicy and smoothly appealing Chardonnay. Ready now.

84 CALLAWAY Chardonnay Temecula Calla-Lees Hawk Watch 1993 **$9.00** Crisp, simple and lively, offering gentle pear and vanilla flavors that linger on the finish. ✪

84 CASTLE ROCK Chardonnay Napa Valley Barrel Fermented 1993 **$10.00** Subtle, polished pear and apple flavors finish with a nutmeg note.

84 CHRISTOPHE Chardonnay North Coast 1993 **$8.00** Serves up ripe pear and apple notes and a touch of toast and spice. Medium in body. ✪

84 CONCANNON Chardonnay Central Coast Selected Vineyard 1993 **$10.00** Well crafted, striking a nice balance between the ripe pear and apple notes and light oak flavors; grassy finish. ✪

84 COTES DE SONOMA Chardonnay Sonoma County 1995 **$9.00** Emphasizes fruit, with green apple and green plum flavors and a lively, almost Muscat-like personality.

84 DE LOACH Chardonnay Sonoma County Sonoma Cuvée 1993 **$10.00** Clean and fruity, with spicy pear, apple and nutmeg notes. Offers a nice value. ✪

84 FETZER Chardonnay North Coast Sundial 1995 **$7.00** Ripe, bright and attractive for its citrusy melon and pear flavors that reman fresh through the finish.

84 FORESTVILLE Chardonnay California 1994 **$6.00** Light, simple and appealing for its almond-scented apple flavors that persist on the smooth finish.

84 LAZY CREEK Chardonnay Anderson Valley 1993 **$10.00** Bright, fresh and spicy, with a resiny edge to the floral apple flavors.

84 MCDOWELL Chardonnay Mendocino 1994 **$10.00** Simple and pleasant enough, delivering a modest range of pear, spice, apple and melon flavors.

84 RAVENSWOOD Chardonnay North Coast Vintners Blend 1993 **$13.00** Tart and flinty, showing a green edge to the pear and apple flavors.

84 RUTHERFORD ESTATE Chardonnay California Barrel Select 1994 **$7.00** Bright and citrusy, a lively mouthful of peach and citrus flavor, softening on the finish. Drinkable now.

84 ST. FRANCIS Chardonnay Sonoma County 1994 **$10.00** A sweet and fruity white that's light and straightforward; a good value at this price. ○

84 SANTA BARBARA WINERY Chardonnay Santa Barbara County 1994 **$9.00** Round and herbal, with pinelike nuances adding to the apple and spice flavors.

84 SEGHESIO Chardonnay Russian River Valley Family Home 1994 **$10.00** Somewhat coarse, featuring spicy pear and vanilla notes. Straightfoward style that's a decent value.

84 SHOOTING STAR Chardonnay Sonoma County 1994 **$10.00** Distinctive for its nectarine and tangerine accents, featuring complex flavors of modest proportions.

84 STEVENOT Chardonnay Calaveras County Reserve 1994 **$10.00** Good intensity, showing pear and peach notes of modest proportions and a strong citrus finish.

84 IVAN TAMAS Chardonnay Livermore Valey Hayes Ranch 1993 **$8.00** Light and pleasantly fruity, generous; its fresh pear and apple flavors linger on the finish. Ready now. ✪

84 TESSERA Chardonnay California 1994 **$9.00** Serves up a modest portion of ripe, spicy pear and hints of oak. Straightforward on the finish. ✪

84 TOAD HOLLOW Chardonnay Russian River Valley Francine's Selection 1994 **$10.00** Openly fruity, with soft pear, apple and spice notes. Simple, but pleasant enough.

84 TREFETHEN Chardonnay Napa Valley Eshcol 1994 **$10.00** Simple, smooth and generous with its juicy apple and spice flavors. Drinkable now. ✪

84 M.G. VALLEJO Chardonnay California 1994 **$6.00** Smooth and flavorful, showing plenty of vanilla-scented pear and citrus character. Ready now.

84 VILLA MT. EDEN Chardonnay California Cellar Select 1994 **$9.00** Crisp and flavorful, with pleasant pear and spice flavors that soften on the finish. ✪

83 BRUTOCAO Chardonnay Mendocino Bliss Vineyard 1993 **$10.00** Spicy, perfumed aroma; elegant and subtle pear and apple notes.

83 CIRRI Chardonnay Sonoma County 1993 **$9.50** Good intensity for the vintage, offering spicy citrus and pear notes that are crisp and clean.

83 DUNNEWOOD Chardonnay Carneros Gold Label Select 1993 **$10.00** A medium-weight, modest, smoky pear edge.

83 GRAND CRU Chardonnay California Premium Selection 1994 **$8.00** Simple and refreshing, with nectarine and citrus flavors lingering briefly on the finish.

83 HIDDEN CELLARS Chardonnay Mendocino County 1993 **$10.00** Pleasant ripe pear, apple and nectarine notes.

83 MONTPELLIER Chardonnay California 1994 **$8.00** A light, simple wine, with pleasant floral and apple flavors. Drinkable now.

83 MORRO BAY Chardonnay Central Coast Special Edition 1994 **$10.00** Has a distinctly earthy edge that hints of celery on top of the sweet apple flavor. It definitely has personality. Drink soon. ✪

83 NAVARRO Chardonnay Anderson Valley 1993 **$8.00** Solid, offering ripe, appealing pear, apple and spice notes. The finish has a light oak shading.

83 NOMINEE Chardonnay Paso Robles 1994 **$7.00** Harmoniously plays its light, smooth spice and fruit flavors off a touch of toasty oak. Ready now. ✪

83 SILVERADO HILL CELLARS Chardonnay Napa Valley Winemaker's Traditional Methode 1994 **$10.00** Distinctive, with a character reminisicent of apple cider that persists on the supple finish.

83 STONE CREEK Chardonnay California
Special Selection 1994 **$7.00** Light and a little
spicy, centered around simple peach fruit that lingers
on the finish. Ready now.

83 TALUS Chardonnay California 1994 **$8.00** A
solid Chardonnay, with ripe, juicy pear, apple and
spice notes. Appealing for its fruitiness. ✪

83 VICHON Chardonnay California Coastal
Selection 1994 **$10.00** Bright, generous and round,
with a spicy edge to the pear fruit. ✪

83 STEPHEN ZELLERBACH Chardonnay
California 1994 **$8.00** A fresh and spicy mouthful
of nectarine, resin and vanilla flavors that soften on
the finish. Drinkable now.

83 CASTLEVIEW Chardonnay Sonoma County
Private Reserve 1993 **$9.00** Light, floral and
appealing, charming for its simple melon and spice
flavors.

82 ROBERT ALISON Chardonnay California
1994 **$6.00** Soft, almost sweet, with a pleasant note
of peach flavor ringing through. Ready now.

82 BLACKSTONE Chardonnay Monterey
County Grand Reserve 1994 **$10.00** Soft and gen-
erous with its citrusy melon flavors that lose a bit of
focus on the finish. Ready now. ✪

82 BOUCHAINE Chardonnay California Q.C.
Fly 1994 **$9.00** Simple and appealing for its fresh,
floral apple flavors.

82 CASTLEVIEW Chardonnay Carneros Private Reserve 1993 **$10.00** Lean, simple and hinting at tasty flavors on the fruity finish. Ready now.

82 CASTORO Chardonnay San Luis Obispo County The Wine 1993 **$10.00** Light and simple, adding a citrus edge to the pear and spice notes.

82 CHRISTOPHE Chardonnay Napa County 1994 **$9.00** Light and a tad earthy, but the bright apple flavor wins in the end.

82 COOPERS' Legacy Chardonnay Sonoma County 1993 **$9.00** Perfumed, ripe pear and honey notes of medium weight.

82 CORBETT CANYON Chardonnay California Coastal Classic 1995 **$6.00** Light and refreshing for its youthful grapefruit and pineapple flavors. ✪

82 J. FRITZ Chardonnay Sonoma County 1993 **$10.00** Marked by grassy tones, this offers a narrow beam of spicy pear flavors in modest proportion.

82 HAWK CREST Chardonnay California 1994 **$9.50** Nice enough, with simple pear, spice and apple notes. Good but nothing exceptional.

82 JEKEL Chardonnay Arroyo Seco Gravelstone Vineyard 1993 **$10.00** Lean and spicy, simple pleasant apple and toast flavors. ✪

82 ROBERT MONDAVI Chardonnay Central Coast Coastal 1994 **$10.00** Ripe and spicy, showing a juicy—almost sweet—core of citrus and grapefruit flavors. ✪

82 MONTHAVEN Chardonnay Napa Valley 1994 **$8.00** Clean and spicy, with a modest core of citrus, pear and spice flavors. A decent wine for the price.

82 SEGHESIO Chardonnay Sonoma County 1993 **$9.00** Crisp, generous spiced apple and vanilla flavors lose a little focus on the finish.

82 SONOMA MISSION Chardonnay Sonoma County 1993 **$8.00** Somewhat lacking in flavor and intensity, but the spicy pear notes dance lightly over the finish.

82 MICHAEL SULLBERG Chardonnay Atlas Peak Lot 55 Barrel Fermented 1991 **$6.00** Mature with an earthy edge to the pear and honey notes, finishing with a slight brackish taste.

82 SUMMERFIELD Chardonnay California Vintner's Reserve 1994 **$8.00** Balances its spicy oak and fresh pear flavors nicely on a medium-bodied frame. ✪

82 IVAN TAMAS Chardonnay Central Coast 1994 **$9.00** Light and bright, offering a nice core of floral and apple flavors. Drinkable now.

82 M.G. VALLEJO Chardonnay California 1993 **$6.00** Smooth and gently spicy, crisp and appley at the core but smooth around the edges, echoing spice on the finish. ✪

81 ARCIERO Chardonnay Paso Robles 1993
$9.00 Has spicy, racy aromas but surprisingly tart
and unyielding in flavor. Drinkable now.

81 BOGLE Chardonnay California Barrel
Fermented Cuvee 1994 **$6.00** A touch earthy, with
hints of pineapple and citrus. Also marked by a lightly
tinny character. ✪

81 CANYON ROAD Chardonnay California
1994 **$7.00** Light, lean and a little grassy behind the
narrow beam of spicy apple flavor. Drinkable now.

81 CHATEAU DE BAUN Chardonnay Russian
River Valley 1994 **$10.00** Simple, ordinary pear
and spice flavors. Good but nothing more.

81 DEER VALLEY Chardonnay Monterey
County 1993 **$7.50** Distinctively spicy in a Muscat
sort of way, broad-textured, showing some bitter
almond and grapefruit on the finish. Drink now.

81 FETZER Chardonnay California Sundial
1993 **$8.00**Smooth and fruity, generous; simple fla-
vors taper on the finish. ✪

81 HACIENDA Chardonnay California Clair de
Lune 1994 **$7.50** Soft, fragrant floral and honey
notes, but a little funky, too, its modest fruit hanging
on the finish. Ready now.

81 HAHN Chardonnay Monterey 1994 **$10.00**
Crisp, simple and appealing, a little short on fruit but
adding citrus notes on the finish.

81 WELLINGTON Chardonnay Sonoma County Barrel Fermented Lot 2 1993 **$8.00** Floral, perfumed, spicy pear and apricot flavors finish with chewy oak notes.

81 WENTE BROS. Chardonnay Central Coast 1994 **$9.00** Light and straightforward, with modest apple and vaguely toasty flavors. Drinkable now. ✪

81 WOODBRIDGE Chardonnay California Barrel Aged 1993 **$6.50** A ripe, fruity earthy edge to the pear and cedary notes. ✪

80 BEAULIEU Chardonnay Napa Valley Beautour 1994 **$9.00** Simple and a little green around the edges of the straightforward apple flavors.

80 CRESTON Chardonnay Paso Robles 1993 **$10.00** Ordinary; simple, grapey pear and citrus notes and a light oak finish.

80 EHLERS GROVE Chardonnay California 1993 **$10.00** Medium-bodied, appealing pear, citrus and light cedary wood flavors.

80 C K MONDAVI Chardonnay California 1994 **$6.00** Soft, fruity and appealing for its snappy tropical fruit and floral flavors. Ready now. ✪

80 MOUNTAIN VIEW Chardonnay Monterey 1993 **$6.50** Light and citrusy, with a strong oaky streak running through the narrow flavors. Ready now.

80 J. PEDRONCELLI Chardonnay Dry Creek Valley **$9.50** Simple, straightforward and spicy, offering a slight tannic bite on the finish.

80 ROSEWOOD Chardonnay Monterey 1994 **$10.00** Ripe, spicy and sturdy, with slightly bitter but solid pineapple and caramel flavors. Second wine of Talbott.

OREGON

87 AUTUMN WIND Chardonnay Oregon 1993 **$10.00** Soft and appealing, displaying youthful pear, citrus and spice flavors gently through the generous finish. Drink it soon.

86 DUCK POND Chardonnay Willamette Valley Barrel Fermented 1994 **$8.00** Youthful, fruity and fresh, like a mouthful of pear. Appealing for its direct fruit flavor.

86 FORIS Chardonnay Rogue Valley Barrel Fermented 1993 **$10.00** Light in texture but shows delicate pear, honey and leafy notes that extend into a smooth finish. Ready now.

85 ASHLAND Chardonnay Rogue Valley Barrel Fermented 1993 **$10.00** Light, spicy and lively with green apple and peppermint flavors that linger nicely on the finish. Ready now.

85 BRIDGEVIEW Chardonnay Oregon 1994 **$6.00** Light and brightly fruity, focusing its spicy apple flavors well into its smooth-textured form. A good and inexpensive white that's drinkable now.

85 HENRY Chardonnay Oregon Umpqua Cuvée 1993 **$9.00** Light in texture and gently fruity, a pleasant wine that opts for lightness over intensity. Tasty now.

85 KNUDSEN ERATH Chardonnay Willamette Valley Erath Vineyards 1994 **$10.00** Fresh and lively, its bright peach and melon flavors coming through the polished veneer. Ready now.

84 AIRLIE Chardonnay Oregon Barrel Fermented 1993 **$10.00** Lean and spicy, with peach-centered fruit that lingers on the smooth finish, touched by the flavor of oak at the end. Ready now.

84 AURORA Chardonnay Willamette Valley 1994 **$8.00** Simple, juicy and refreshing, a mouthful of pear, apple and resiny flavors that linger on the lively finish.

84 EOLA HILLS Chardonnay Oregon 1994 **$9.00** Simple, crisp and lively with apple and spice flavors, finishing with a touch of cream to smooth it out. Ready now.

84 MONTINORE Chardonnay Willamette Valley 1993 **$9.00** Balanced toward fruit, a juicy mouthful of citrus, honey and pear flavors that linger on the finish. Drinkable now.

84 TUALATIN Chardonnay Willamette Valley Barrel Fermented 1993 **$10.00** Light in texture and balanced toward fruit, with green apple and melon flavors finishing crisply.

83 HINMAN VINEYARDS Chardonnay Oregon 1994 **$10.00** Fresh, fruity and appealing, brimming with pear and citrus flavors that remain juicy through the finish. Ready now.

Washington

88 W.B. BRIDGMAN Chardonnay Yakima Valley 1993 **$9.00** Smooth and rich, sporting a distinct black pepper and dusky spice undertone to the buttery pear flavors. Drink now.

88 COLUMBIA CREST Chardonnay Columbia Valley Barrel Select 1993 **$10.00** Smooth and lively, butterscotch flavors yielding ultimately to zingy citrus and ripe pear on the harmonious finish. Delicious now.

88 HOGUE Chardonnay Columbia Valley 1994 **$9.00** A smooth and spicy white from Washington that's nicely balanced to show off its pineapple, pear and nutmeg flavors. The finish lingers pleasantly, and this looks good for its value, too. Drinkable now. ✪

87 BOOKWALTER Chardonnay Washington 1994 **$9.00** Ripe and round, spicy around the edges, offering pear and toasty vanilla flavors at the core and a firm texture. Drink now.

87 CATERINA Chardonnay Columbia Valley 1994 **$10.00** Smooth and gentle in texture, featuring lively, juicy citrus and pear flavors that linger on the finish.

87 CHERRY HILL Chardonnay Columbia Valley 1994 **$6.00** Focused, lively, resiny pear and vanilla flavors remain zingy through the finish, folding in a touch of oak.

87 COASTAL CELLARS Chardonnay Yakima Valley 1993 **$6.00** Remarkably fresh and spicy, the core of nectarine and apple flavors shines through, and the finish is crisp and focused.

87 POWERS Chardonnay Columbia Valley 1993 **$8.00** Bright and brimming with apple, vanilla and citrus flavors. Ready now.

87 WATERBROOK Chardonnay Columbia Valley 1994 **$10.00** A bright, ripe and fruity Washington white that offers good flavors for the dollars. A nice thread of spicy oak runs through this to balance it out. Drinkable now.

86 BADGER MOUNTAIN Chardonnay Columbia Valley Certified Organic Vineyard 1994 **$9.00** Light, bright, lively green apple, pear and spice flavors maintain vibrancy through the finish.

85 PAUL THOMAS Chardonnay Washington 1994 **$9.00** Bright and resiny, a mouthful of green apple and pine flavors that are distinctive and fresh. Drinkable now. ✪

84 BADGER MOUNTAIN Chardonnay Columbia Valley Certified Organic Vineyard 1993 **$9.00** Smooth, refreshing, lively citrus and pear flavors plus a touch of oak on the finish.

84 COLUMBIA CREST Chardonnay Columbia Valley 1994 **$8.00** Light, juicy peach and apple flavors, smooth texture. Drinkable now. ✪

84 HYATT Chardonnay Yakima Valley 1993 **$8.00** Crisp, spicy and sharply focused, leaning a little toward oak for flavor but there's a nice, citrusy bite to the finish. Drinkable now.

84 MARBLE CREST Chardonnay Columbia Valley 1993 **$8.00** Tasty and bright, adding a spicy edge to the pear flavor that keeps flowing generously on the finish.

84 SILVER LAKE Chardonnay Columbia Valley Sentinel Peak 1993 **$7.00** Lean and spicy, crisp in texture, as citrusy pear and floral flavors extend into a lively finish.

83 SILVER LAKE Chardonnay Columbia Valley 1993 **$8.50** Supple, generous up front and dripping with pear and citrusy flavors, narrowing a bit on the finish.

83 TUCKER Chardonnay Yakima Valley 1992 **$10.00** Smooth and appealing, modest in scope, showing spicy pear and orange flavors weaving through the soft finish.

82 POWERS Chardonnay Columbia Valley 1994 **$8.00** Light and spicy, sneaking some toasty oak into the mix on the finish.

OTHER U.S.

83 WAGNER Chardonnay Finger Lakes Grace House 1993 **$10.00** Toasty oak notes are pleasant, if dominant, but there's enough green apple flavor to carry this crisp, round white through a clean finish.

81 BILTMORE ESTATE Chardonnay North Carolina Sur Lies 1993 **$9.00** Straightforward and well balanced, rather austere, offering pear, melon and toast flavors, good acidity and a clean finish. It would be fine with food.

Chenin Blanc

CALIFORNIA

86 CHAPPELLET Chenin Blanc Napa Valley Dry 1994 **$9.00** Crisp and flavorful, a dry wine with pretty apple and spice flavors that linger on the finish.

84 BONNY DOON Chenin Blanc California Pacific Rim 1994 **$8.00** Bright and fresh, bubbling with youthful grapey and citric flavors, finishing soft but dry.

83 DRY CREEK Chenin Blanc Clarksburg Dry 1994 **$7.00** Soft, spicy apple and almond flavors are pleasant to drink soon.

82 DANIEL GEHRS Chenin Blanc Monterey County Le Cheniere Carmel Vineyard 1994 **$8.00** Dry and flavorful, with a profile like apple cider and a light finish.

WASHINGTON

85 KIONA Chenin Blanc Yakima Valley 1994
$6.00 Bright and fruity, off-dry and focused, featuring pear and almond flavors that swirl nicely on the finish.

84 COLUMBIA Chenin Blanc Yakima Valley 1994 **$6.00** Soft and effusively fruity, a gentle white offering lots of appealing pear flavor and a slightly floral finish.

84 HOGUE Chenin Blanc Columbia Valley 1994 **$6.00** Fresh, fruity and appealing, off-dry and richened by peach and melon flavors.

84 HOGUE Chenin Blanc Columbia Valley Dry 1994 **$6.00** Melon and pear flavors linger on the off-dry finish in this light and somewhat resiny Chenin.

83 LATAH CREEK Chenin Blanc Washington 1994 **$6.00** Sweet but balanced with lemony acidity, centered around pear and apple flavors. Ready now.

82 PONTIN DEL ROZA Chenin Blanc Columbia Valley 1995 **$6.00** Soft and pleasant. Slightly sweet pear and almond flavors. Drink it soon.

Gewürztraminer

CALIFORNIA

87 CLAIBORNE & CHURCHILL Gewürztraminer Central Coast Dry Alsatian Style 1994 **$10.00** Soft and effusively fruity, but dry, unfolding its black pepper, spice and orange cream flavors elegantly. Ready now.

86 GEYSER PEAK Gewürztraminer California 1995 **$7.00** Soft and generous with its pineapple, citrus, honeysuckle and spice flavors, and it finishes characteristically for this variety, off-dry and round. A definite good value.

84 GUNDLACH BUNDSCHU Gewürztraminer Sonoma Valley 1994 **$9.00** Dry but distinctly fruity, centering its flavors around peach and melon. Not much to say Gewurz, but a nice sipping wine.

83 MILL CREEK Gewürztraminer North Coast 1994 **$8.00** Soft, off-dry and appealing for its rose petal fragrance and light pear notes.

81 BOUCHAINE Gewürztraminer Russian River Valley Dry 1994 **$8.50** Soft in texture but dry and floral, a light wine with more rose petal than fruit flavor.

80 LAWRENCE J. BARGETTO Gewürztraminer Santa Cruz Mountains Barrel Fermented Dry 1994 **$10.00** Has pretty fruit and spice up front that fades quickly but offers a nice zip before it disappears. Ready now.

Oregon

87 MONTINORE Gewürztraminer Willamette Valley 1993 **$6.00** Lightly sweet and fragrant, offering spicy pear and grapefruit flavors that linger delicately on the finish. Drinkable now.

84 AIRLIE Gewürztraminer Oregon 1994 **$6.50** Smooth texture, floral flavors and clean, dry finish make this an easy wine to like.

84 FORIS Gewürztraminer Rogue Valley 1994 **$8.00** Fresh and inviting, dry and ever-so-slightly bitter, but the characteristic spicy fruit wins in the end.

83 HENRY Gewürztraminer Umpqua Valley Dry 1994 **$8.00** Off dry, with generous apricot-scented spice and pear flavors that lean toward spiciness on the finish. Ready now.

83 TUALATIN Gewürztraminer Willamette Valley 1993 **$6.00** Distinctively varietal, spicy and refreshing, but the bitterness shows through the dry finish. Try in 1997.

80 BRIDGEVIEW Gewürztraminer Oregon 1993 **$6.00** Soft and generally fruity, but not specifically varietal. Pleasant now.

WASHINGTON

86 TUCKER Gewürztraminer Yakima Valley 1994 **$6.00** Lightly sweet and appealingly flavorful, weaving spicy rose petal overtones through the pear and apricot notes. Drink now.

85 COLUMBIA Gewürztraminer Yakima Valley 1995 **$6.00** Frankly sweet, with a delicate rose petal note persisting from first whiff to the finish, echoing pear and honey.

85 WASHINGTON HILLS Gewürztraminer Columbia Valley Varietal Select 1994 **$7.00** Remarkably fresh and vibrant, off-dry, like biting into a fresh peach with lovely spice and floral overtones.

83 HOGUE Gewürztraminer Columbia Valley 1994 **$6.00** Soft and floral, frankly sweet and full of appealing pear and spice flavors.

83 HOODSPORT Gewürztraminer Washington 1994 **$8.00** Bright and fruity and off-dry, a mouthful of fresh pear and delicate floral overtones.

83 SNOQUALMIE Gewürztraminer Columbia Valley 1994 **$6.00** A little sweet but nicely balanced to show off the nectarine and delicate rose petal flavors.

82 PAUL THOMAS Gewürztraminer Columbia Valley 1994 **$6.00** Soft and simple, appealing for its pretty pear and honey flavors.

80 COLUMBIA CREST Gewürztraminer
Columbia Valley 1995 **$6.00** Sweet, citrusy flavors
show little Gewürztraminer character, but this makes a
pleasant sipper. ✪

Pinot Blanc

CALIFORNIA

84 DANIEL GEHRS Pinot Blanc Monterey
County Carmel Vineyard 1994 **$10.00** Simple,
earthy edge to the vanilla and pear flavors. Succeeds
in its delicacy and finesse.

82 LOCKWOOD Pinot Blanc Monterey 1993
$9.00 Ripe, round and spicy, sturdy rather than sup-
ple, finishing with concentrated flavor.

80 PARAISO SPRINGS Pinot Blanc Santa Lucia
Highlands 1994 **$9.00** Very spicy style, with more
oak apparent than fruit, finishing smooth.

Pinot Gris

OREGON

85 EOLA HILLS Pinot Gris Oregon 1994 **$10.00**
Ripe and generous, soft around the edges, but it shows
off its citrusy melon and almond flavors with flair.
Drinkable now.

84 BRIDGEVIEW Pinot Gris Oregon Cuvée
Speciale 1994 **$10.00** Soft and fruity, centered
around pear and almond flavors, and a wee bit smoky
on the finish. Drinkable now.

83 MONTINORE Pinot Gris Willamette Valley 1994 **$10.00** A light, fresh and simple white that puts a spicy spin on its pear flavor.

Riesling

CALIFORNIA

88 BONNY DOON Riesling California Pacific Rim 1994 **$8.00** A stylishly delicate, dry and fragrant white that offers varietal character in a value package. Throws out peach, floral and citrus flavors that linger appealingly on the finish.

87 GAINEY Johannisberg Riesling Santa Ynez Valley 1994 **$8.50** Lightly sweet, delicate in texture, but rich with apricot-scented pear flavors. Drinkable now.

85 GEYSER PEAK Johannisberg Riesling North Coast Soft 1994 **$6.00** A fresh, youthful style, lightly sweet and showing exuberant peach and floral flavors. Finishes with a touch of a resiny quality. Great price, too. ✪

85 QUAFF White Riesling Monterey County 1993 **$7.50** Light and lively, just off-dry, sporting orange, apple and vanilla flavors. Ready now.

85 TREFETHEN Riesling Napa Valley Dry 1994 **$9.75** Smells fruity and open, an off-dry white turning toward lime and floral notes on the tart finish.

85 VENTANA Riesling Monterey Dry 1994 **$6.00** Light and fragrant, a zesty mouthful of apple, floral and peppery flavors that linger appealingly on the finish.

84 CLAIBORNE & CHURCHILL Riesling Central Coast Dry Alsatian Style 1994 **$10.00** Tart and citrusy, light enough to be a refreshing apéritif.

84 GREENWOOD RIDGE White Riesling Anderson Valley 1994 **$8.50** Soft and creamy in texture, lightly sweet, with a delicate vanilla note floating over the gentle pear flavors.

84 VENTANA Johannisberg Riesling Monterey 1994 **$6.00** Delicately sweet, with modest apricot and apple flavors with pine-like overtones. A nice sipper.

New York

88 HERMANN J. WIEMER Johannisberg Riesling Finger Lakes Semi-Dry 1994 **$10.00** Floral and honey aromas are intriguing, and follow through on the vibrant palate with attractive peach and lime flavors. It's firm, delicate and nicely balanced. A great-value Riesling.

85 GLENORA Riesling Finger Lakes Dry 1994 **$8.00** Delicate floral and citrus aromas and flavors give this a light, Mosel-like character, offering peach notes that linger on the finish.

84 DR. KONSTANTIN FRANK Johannisberg Riesling Finger Lakes Semi-Dry 1994 **$9.00** An easy-drinking wine with apple, peach and pine flavors, plus enough sweetness to round out any hard edges. Clean and straightforward.

84 HERMANN J. WIEMER Johannisberg Riesling Finger Lakes Dry 1994 **$8.50** This pleasantly fruity white shows typical Riesling flavors of peach, mineral and light herbs. It's full-bodied yet dry and well balanced.

83 LAMOREAUX LANDING Riesling Finger Lakes Dry 1994 **$8.00** Generous aromas of mango and lime give way to a more austere palate and steely acidity. It's clean and refreshing.

81 SWEDISH HILL Johannisberg Riesling Finger Lakes 1992 **$8.00** An appealing, straightforward, smooth-textured and sweet Riesling with apple and citrus flavors and a touch of vanilla on the finish.

80 WAGNER Johannisberg Riesling Finger Lakes 1994 **$8.00** The Riesling character of peaches is there but a bit diluted, and the full-bodied wine needs more acidity to balance the sweetness.

OREGON

87 VAN DUZER Riesling Dry Oregon Reserve 1994 **$8.00** Distinctly and attractively varietal, as peach, floral and spice flavors mingle nicely through the racy finish. Ready now.

86 ARGYLE Riesling Dry Oregon Reserve 1993 **$9.00** Feels sweet but finishes in a nice zap of citrusy acidity to balance the ripe apricot flavor. Ready now.

85 KNUDSEN ERATH Riesling Willamette Valley 1994 **$7.00** Soft, sweet, generous nectarine, honeysuckle and pear flavors echo nicely on the finish.

85 WILLAMETTE VALLEY Riesling Oregon Dry 1994 **$8.00** Bright and lively with apricot-scented peach and apple flavors, generous and fresh.

84 ASHLAND Riesling Oregon Dry 1994 **$5.00** Soft and fruity, weaving some honey flavors through the peachy character and somewhat intense finish. Ready now.

83 BRIDGEVIEW Riesling Oregon Blue Moon Limited Edition NV **$6.00** Simple, soft, fruity and appealing, a nice mouthful of melon and peach. A value for everyday drinking. ✪

83 MONTINORE White Riesling Willamette Valley 1993 **$6.00** Soft and fragrant, showing a strong pinelike quality to the floral peach and melon flavors. Drinkable now.

82 TUALATIN Riesling Willamette Valley 1994 **$5.00** Sweet and simple, nectarine flavors lasting into a light finish.

81 SILVAN RIDGE Riesling Willamette Valley Forgeron Vineyard Dry 1993 **$8.00** Very pretty, floral aromas, but its resiny flavors take some getting used to. Dry enough to enjoy with food. Ready now.

80 AIRLIE Riesling Oregon 1994 **$6.50** Lightly sweet and spicy, simple but appealing. Ready now.

WASHINGTON

87 SNOQUALMIE Johannisberg Riesling Columbia Valley 1993 **$6.00** A bright and immaculate Washington white that shows off its peach, pear and zippy citrus flavors as they sail smoothly through the finish. Utterly beguiling for its taste and price.

86 KIONA White Riesling Columbia Valley 1994 **$6.00** Vibrant and refreshing, with exciting floral, peach and apple flavors; a classic off-dry Riesling for summer sipping.

86 SNOQUALMIE Johannisberg Riesling Columbia Valley Dry 1994 **$6.00** Generous, harmonious and spilling over with fruit, offering nectarine, pear and a hint of floral spice. Enjoy it now.

86 WASHINGTON HILLS Johannisberg Riesling Columbia Valley Varietal Select 1994 **$7.00** Smooth and lightly sweet; generous peach, pear and delicate pine flavors. Drink while it is fresh.

85 HOODSPORT Johannisberg Riesling Washington 1994 **$8.00** Smells and tastes like crushed wildflowers, adding a touch of nectarine on the finish.

85 HOGUE Johannisberg Riesling Columbia Valley Dry 1994 **$6.00** Fresh and faintly sweet, like biting into a green apple, adding some apricot on the finish. Ready now. ✪

85 SEVEN HILLS White Riesling Columbia Valley 1995 **$7.00** Off-dry, bright and lively, with disarmingly fresh peach and floral flavors.

84 COLUMBIA CREST Johannisberg Riesling Columbia Valley 1995 **$6.00** Brightly aromatic, with a rush of apple and floral aromas that become soft and less lively on the palate. A pleasant sipper from Washington that's easy on the wallet. ✪

84 SNOQUALMIE Johannisberg Riesling Columbia Valley 1994 **$6.00** Light and somewhat tart, citrusy, showing appealing floral and apple flavor and a touch of sweetness. Ready now.

84 STEWART Johannisberg Riesling Columbia Valley 1994 **$5.50** Fresh, off-dry, fruity and bright, featuring Golden Delicious apple and floral flavors. Drink now.

84 PAUL THOMAS Johannisberg Riesling Columbia Valley Dry 1994 **$6.00** Light and charming, rolling out its peach, apricot and apple flavors with finesse.

84 WASHINGTON HILLS Riesling Columbia Valley Varietal Select Dry 1993 **$6.00** Lean, light and gently fruity, echoing green apple and peach flavors on the finish. Just off-dry.

84 YAKIMA RIVER Johannisberg Riesling Yakima Valley 1995 **$6.50** Fresh apple and peach flavors are soft and appealing.

83 COLUMBIA Johannisberg Riesling Columbia Valley 1994 **$6.00** Lightly sweet and generous apricot, peach and apple flavors and a refreshing touch of orange peel on the finish.

83 COVEY RUN Johannisberg Riesling Yakima Valley 1994 **$7.00** Fruity and lightly sweet, accenting peach and vanilla.

83 COVEY RUN Riesling Columbia Valley Dry 1994 **$7.00** Soft and fruity, adding a resiny edge to the pear and peach flavors.

82 COLUMBIA Johannisberg Riesling Columbia Valley Cellarmaster's Reserve 1994 **$6.50** A little sugary, offering nice pear and honey notes.

81 KIONA White Riesling Yakima Valley Dry 1994 **$6.00** Light and appealing, a delicate white showing modest peach and resin flavors.

80 LATAH CREEK Johannisberg Riesling Washington 1994 **$6.00** Simple, fruity and refreshing, lightly sweet, featuring pear and floral flavors.

80 PAUL THOMAS Johannisberg Riesling Columbia Valley 1994 **$6.00** Soft and simple, offering appealing pear and slightly floral flavors.

OTHER U.S.

80 OASIS Riesling Virginia 1992 **$8.00** There are pleasant elements here—apple and piney flavors, an easy balance of light sweetness and lemony acidity—but some earthy and candied notes detract slightly.

Sauvignon Blanc

C ALIFORNIA

90 BERNARDUS Sauvignon Blanc Monterey County 1994 **$10.00** Bright and pure, pouring out its generous pear, pineapple and citrus flavors. An incredible value in a California white that's fresh and lively through the long finish. Delicious now.

89 GEYSER PEAK Sauvignon Blanc Sonoma County 1995 **$8.00** The zingy, citrusy flavors show delicious shadings of passion fruit, lemongrass and spice, making for a lively, distinctive white to drink soon. Can't argue with the price either.

89 SHENANDOAH Sauvignon Blanc Amador County 1995 **$8.00** Bright and nimble, an invigorating mouthful of passion fruit, citrus and fig flavors that keep swirling through the finish.

88 BEAULIEU Sauvignon Blanc Napa Valley 1994 **$8.00** Strongly floral, with rose petal and anise scents. Pear flavors finish with lively intensity.

88 CASK ONE Sauvignon Blanc Mendocino County 1994 **$6.00** Crisp and lively. Sharply focused pear, green apple and herbal flavors are balanced and refreshing.

88 MAYACAMAS Sauvignon Blanc Napa Valley 1993 **$10.00** Clean and crisp, boasting pretty pear, spice, citrus and floral notes. Altogether elegant and refreshing; ideal for summertime.

88 STEPHEN ZELLERBACH Sauvignon Blanc Sonoma County 1993 **$7.00** This is frankly herbal and shows distinctively varietal character in its aromas, but it rounds out the flavors with soft, charming pear and apple—a fine balance that enhances its value.

87 ARCIERO Sauvignon Blanc Paso Robles 1994 **$6.00** Soft and generous with its passion fruit, peach and pear flavors, smooth and appealing to drink now.

87 BUENA VISTA Sauvignon Blanc Lake County 1995 **$8.00** Light-bodied, with a welcome crispness that complements the melon and citrus flavors.

87 FETZER Fumé Blanc Mendocino County 1993 **$7.00** Appealing, bright pear and apple flavors are shaded nicely by touches of herb and celery. The fruit wins out on the finish. Good value. ✪

87 GREENWOOD RIDGE Sauvignon Blanc Anderson Valley 1994 **$9.00** Bright and citrusy, a nice mouthful of grapefruit, peach and herb. Easy-drinking and appealing.

87 HANDLEY Sauvignon Blanc Dry Creek Valley 1993 **$9.00** Ripe, nicely focused pear, spice and a touch of herb; beautifully balanced style that centers around fruit.

87 HANNA Sauvignon Blanc Sonoma County 1994 **$10.00** Bright and fruity. Snappy, vibrant anise-scented pear and vanilla flavors.

87 HUSCH Sauvignon Blanc Mendocino 1994
$9.00 Light and juicy, a nice mouthful of passion
fruit, grapefruit and pineapple flavor that persists on
the lively finish.

87 JEPSON Sauvignon Blanc Mendocino
County Estate Select 1994 **$8.50** Smooth and
juicy, with some nice peppery notes wrapped in a ripe
nectarine package. Drinkable now.

87 KENWOOD Sauvignon Blanc Sonoma
County 1994 **$9.50** A fresh and lively value of a
Sauvignon Blanc. This offers a mouthful of grape-
fruit, pear and subtle herb flavors. Delicious now.

87 LAKEWOOD Sauvignon Blanc Clear Lake
1994 **$10.00** Bright, crisp and disarming for its live-
ly green apple, fennel and spice flavors that linger on
the finish. Ready now.

87 LOCKWOOD Sauvignon Blanc Monterey
1995 **$10.00** Mouth-filling butterscotch, citrus and
herb flavors seem a little raucous at this point, but the
crisp finish brings it together nicely.

87 MARKHAM Sauvignon Blanc Napa Valley
1994 **$8.00** Bright and focused, showing lots of sweet
tropical fruit, floral and herb flavors that swirl through
the finish. A good value for immediate enjoyment. ✪

87 MURPHY-GOODE Fumé Blanc Alexander
Valley 1994 **$10.00** Light and smooth, its vibrant
nectarine and spice flavors humming nicely on the
finish. Not much that says Sauvignon, but tasty and
long. ✪

87 CHATEAU POTELLE Sauvignon Blanc Napa Valley 1994 **$9.50** Light, crisp, refreshing tropical fruit and citrusy flavors that linger.

87 RANCHO SISQUOC Sauvignon Blanc Santa Maria Valley 1993 **$10.00** Definitely wrapped in a layer of sweet oak. Ripe and spicy; balanced and fruity enough to stay lively through the finish.

87 RENAISSANCE Sauvignon Blanc North Yuba 1994 **$9.00** Pear and grassy flavors that are typical of this varietal. Earthy, spicy and floral notes add flair and complexity.

87 RUTHERFORD VINEYARDS Fumé Blanc Napa Valley 1993 **$8.00** Bright, citrusy, lively; generous peach, apple and grapefruit flavors remain fresh through the finish.

87 CHATEAU ST. JEAN Fumé Blanc Sonoma County 1994 **$8.00** Ripe and refreshing, delivering complex herb, citrus and fig flavors. Drinkable now. ✪

87 VOSS Sauvignon Blanc Napa Valley 1994 **$9.00** Ripe and flavorful, the pear and apple nuances laced with distinctly varietal, floral-grassy character. Tasty finish.

86 BOGLE Fumé Blanc California 1994 **$5.00** Focused and fruity, this Sauvignon Blanc has bright pear, nectarine and modestly herbal flavors swirling through its smooth, sturdy texture. A fair price for this kind of character, which makes it all the easier to enjoy now.

86 COTES DE SONOMA Sauvignon Blanc
Sonoma County 1995 **$9.00** Bright and flavorful,
an appealing wine brimming with melon, vanilla and
green berry flavors.

86 FETZER Fumé Blanc Mendocino County
1995 **$6.00** A mouthful of vivid, fruit flavors—crisp
apple, citrus and peach—that have just a hint of herb.

86 MILL CREEK Sauvignon Blanc Dry Creek
Valley 1994 **$8.00** Smooth and spicy, balancing
crisp grapefruit against spicy oak in a light- to medi-
um-weight wine.

86 NAPA RIDGE Sauvignon Blanc North Coast
Coastal 1994 **$5.00** A bright and crisp California
white that folds in some lively herbal aromas and flavors to go along with the citrus and melon notes.
Drinkable now, and what an attractive price. ✪

86 J. PEDRONCELLI Fumé Blanc Dry Creek
Valley 1994 **$8.50** Fruity and floral, with citrus
and pear flavors. Some zingy herb and chocolate (!)
overtones.

86 QUIVIRA Sauvignon Blanc Dry Creek Valley
1994 **$10.00** Bright, crisp and lively with pear, spice
and a hint of celery. Ready now.

86 SILVERADO Sauvignon Blanc Napa Valley
1995 **$10.00** Ripe, mouth-filling and flavorful; a
core of pear, citrus and smoky flavors and a smooth,
round finish. ✪

86 RODNEY STRONG Sauvignon Blanc Northern Sonoma Charlotte's Home Vineyard 1995 **$10.00** Bright and citrusy, nicely polished to show off its nectarine and grapefruit flavors.

85 ALDERBROOK Sauvignon Blanc Dry Creek Valley 1994 **$8.50** Plays its lively pear and green apple against a nice thread of spicy oak, weaving touches of herb through it all.

85 BOGLE Fumé Blanc California Dry 1994 **$5.50** Light and appealing for its upple peach and green apple fruit, hinting at mint on the finish. Ready now.

85 FETZER Sauvignon Blanc North Coast Barrel Select 1994 **$10.00** Light-bodied and crisp. Has citrusy apple flavors with a distinctly herbal tang.

85 FLORA SPRINGS Sauvignon Blanc Napa Valley 1993 **$8.00** Straightforward, soft and fruity; pleasant pear flavors and a flash of spice on the finish.

85 FOPPIANO Sauvignon Blanc Dry Creek Valley 1993 **$8.50** Focuses its ripe, generous pear and citrusy orange flavors into a lively finish. Somewhat hot at the end, but ready now.

85 GEYSER PEAK Sauvignon Blanc Sonoma County 1994 **$7.50** A lean and lively white that's distinctive for adding anise and herbal overtones to the basic apple and kiwi flavors. ✪

85 HAWK CREST Sauvignon Blanc California 1994 **$8.00** Bright and fruity, appealing for its clear apple and citrus flavors. Ready now.

85 HIDDEN CELLARS Sauvignon Blanc Mendocino 1994 **$9.00** Soft and pleasantly fruity, adding a tobacco edge to the lingering citrus and peach flavors. Ready now.

85 MIRASSOU Sauvignon Blanc California 1993 **$6.00** Soft and simple, showing nice grapefruit and floral flavors that linger on the finish. ✪

85 MORO VINO Sauvignon Blanc Santa Barbara County 1995 **$10.00** Tart, crisp and tangy, with citrusy herbal flavors that hold on through a zingy finish.

85 MOUNT KONOCTI Fumé Blanc Lake County 1994 **$8.00** Bright and tasty, generous with its pear, papaya and spice flavors and hinting at honey on the finish.

85 QUIVIRA Sauvignon Blanc Dry Creek Valley 1993 **$10.00** Light and fragrant, more floral than herbal, offering citrusy flavors on the finish.

85 RAYMOND Sauvignon Blanc Napa Valley Reserve 1995 **$10.00** Bright and fruity pear and floral flavors with a smoky accent.

85 ROUND HILL Fumé Blanc Napa Valley 1993 **$7.00** Immediately appealing peach and vanilla flavors linger in this bright, fruity, exuberant white.

85 SEGHESIO Sauvignon Blanc Sonoma County 1994 **$9.00** Light, lean and lively; bright pear and floral flavors.

85 CHATEAU SOUVERAIN Sauvignon Blanc Alexander Valley Barrel Fermented 1994 **$8.00** Lean and lively, flavors centered around nectarine, grapefruit and a touch of grass.

85 STERLING Sauvignon Blanc Napa Valley 1995 **$8.00** Crisp and appealing for its bright apple, vanilla and grapefruit flavors that linger nicely on the finish.

85 VENTANA Sauvignon Blanc Monterey 1994 **$9.00** Soft and appealing, a nice mouthful of bright pear and apple flavors. Drinkable now.

84 AUDUBON Sauvignon Blanc Napa Valley Juliana Vineyards 1994 **$9.00** Lean and focused, tobacco and cedar notes accenting the pear flavor.

84 BERINGER Sauvignon Blanc Napa Valley 1993 **$8.50** Buttery, spicy and round, a generous wine that's less Sauvignon than Chardonnay—and a pretty good one, if somewhat woody. ✪

84 BYINGTON Sauvignon Blanc San Luis Obispo County French Camp Vineyard 1993 **$8.00** A spicy feeling runs through the honeysuckle and pear flavors. Crisp and peppery.

84 CLOS DU BOIS Sauvignon Blanc Sonoma County 1994 **$8.00** Very fresh, lively and bright, showing apple and floral flavors. ✪

84 DRY CREEK Fumé Blanc Sonoma County Dry 1993 **$9.50** Simple, sturdy and nicely focused, showing pear and green, leafy notes. ✪

84 HAVENS Sauvignon Blanc Napa Valley Clock Vineyard 1994 **$10.00** Smooth and fruity, featuring nectarine, spice and slightly grassy and vanilla overtones.

84 KENDALL-JACKSON Sauvignon Blanc California Vintner's Reserve 1995 **$10.00** Fresh and citrusy. A lively wine with refreshing grapefruit and floral flavors.

84 ROBERT PECOTA Sauvignon Blanc Napa Valley 1995 **$7.50** Round and flavorful. Pear flavors have a strong herbal-weedy edge that persists through the finish.

84 R.H. PHILLIPS Sauvignon Blanc Dunnigan Hills Night Harvest 1995 **$5.50** Open-textured and bright. Pear and vanilla flavors gain a hint of herb on the finish.

84 SHENANDOAH Sauvignon Blanc Amador County 1994 **$7.50** Definitely floral and herbal, a soft, round-textured white that adds a noticeable dose of oak on the finish.

84 SIMI Sauvignon Blanc Sonoma County 1993 **$9.00** Soft and fruity, offering a floral edge to the slightly honeyed pear flavors. ✪

84 IVAN TAMAS Sauvignon Blanc Livermore Valley Figoni Ranch 1994 **$9.00** Frankly varietal, with anise and celery flavors weaving through the bright, citrusy fruit. Drink it soon.

83 BANDIERA Sauvignon Blanc Napa Valley 1994 **$5.50** Crisp and generally fruity, hinting at nectarine and a touch of herb on the finish.

83 COTES DE SONOMA Sauvignon Blanc Sonoma County 1994 **$7.00** A crisp and lively touch of floral character spikes up the green apple and green berry flavors.

83 CRESTON Sauvignon Blanc Paso Robles 1995 **$10.00** Ripe and a bit thick in texture, but pleasant for its peach and apple flavors.

83 FIELD STONE Sauvignon Blanc Sonoma County 1994 **$9.00** Smooth and fruity, nicely balanced to show its pear and peppery spice flavors.

83 J. FRITZ Sauvignon Blanc Dry Creek Valley 1994 **$9.50** Solid and flavorful, featuring generous pear, spice and slightly herbal notes.

83 GRAND CRU Sauvignon Blanc California 1994 **$7.00** Soft and floral, with a nice hint of peach on the finish.

83 GROTH Sauvignon Blanc Napa Valley 1994 **$9.00** Lean and definitely herbal, showing an onion-skin edge to the peppery pear flavors.

83 KENWOOD Sauvignon Blanc Sonoma County 1995 **$9.50** Simple and direct, with appealing citrus and spicy nectarine flavors. ✪

83 CHARLES B. MITCHELL Sauvignon Blanc El Dorado 1993 **$6.00** Soft, generous vanilla-scented pear and slightly leafy green berry flavors.

83 ROBERT MONDAVI Sauvignon Blanc North Coast Coastal 1994 **$9.00** Floral, oddly foxy flavors characterize this soft, lightly citrusy white. Ready now. ✪

83 MONTHAVEN Sauvignon Blanc Napa Valley 1994 **$6.00** A crisp white marked by a core of grassy citrus, lemon and herb flavors. Elegant and refined; easy-drinking.

83 R.H. PHILLIPS Sauvignon Blanc Night Harvest 1994 **$5.50** Light and simple, offering a nice core of apple and spice flavors. ✪

83 SANTA BARBARA WINERY Sauvignon Blanc Santa Ynez Valley 1993 **$8.00** Accented by rose petal and herb flavors, this keeps a solid core of pear and ginger floating through the finish.

83 WILDHURST Sauvignon Blanc Clear Lake 1994 **$9.00** Fruity and straightforward with its anise-scented grapefruit and melon flavors.

82 ALDERBROOK Sauvignon Blanc Dry Creek Valley 1993 **$8.50** Soft, generous spicy orange and pear flavors.

82 DAVIS BYNUM Fumé Blanc Russian River Valley Shone Farm Dry 1994 **$8.50** Appealing for its simple pear and gooseberry flavors.

82 ESTANCIA Sauvignon Blanc Monterey 1994 **$8.00** Broad and spicy, adding an undertone of vegetal flavors that sneak through the modest pear and toast on the finish.

82 J. FURST Fumé Blanc California 1991 **$9.00**
An herbal-smelling, green-tasting Sauvignon with flavors of green bean, tarragon and lemon. It's fresh and bracing, with decent fruit flavors and touch of toasty flavor presumably from oak aging.

82 GLEN ELLEN Fumé Blanc California Proprietor's Reserve 1994 **$6.00** Light, spicy, with a vanilla edge to the modest citrus flavors.

82 JEPSON Sauvignon Blanc Mendocino 1993 **$8.50** Smooth and refreshing, lively and fruity enough to show off the mildly herbal pear flavors; soft finish.

82 JOLIESSE VINEYARDS Sauvignon Blanc California Reserve 1994 **$7.00** Generous herb and sweet pear flavors make this a pleasant, easy-to-drink wine. ○

82 KENDALL-JACKSON Sauvignon Blanc California Vintner's Reserve 1994 **$9.50** Light, lean and somewhat sweet, finishing with a floral flourish and delicate vanilla notes.

82 KUNDE Sauvignon Blanc Sonoma Valley Magnolia Lane 1994 **$10.00** Toasted onion notes waft through the green pear flavors in this smooth and distinctly herbal white. Ready now.

82 CHARLES B. MITCHELL Fumé Blanc El Dorado 1994 **$7.50** Pear and spice flavors are soft, fruity and pleasant.

82 MONTEREY VINEYARD Sauvignon Blanc Central Coast Classic 1994 **$5.50** Crisp and floral; some wood flavor shows through the modest fruit.

82 RUTHERFORD ESTATE Sauvignon Blanc Napa Valley 1992 **$6.00** Light and smooth, offering a mild vanilla edge to the herbal pear notes.

82 CHATEAU ST. JEAN Fumé Blanc Sonoma County Dry 1993 **$8.00** Straightforward, a sturdy white featuring simple pear flavor and hints of spice on the finish. **✪**

82 SANFORD Sauvignon Blanc Santa Barbara County 1993 **$9.50** Smooth, supple, modest fruit flavors pop through on the finish.

82 M.G. VALLEJO Sauvignon Blanc California 1993 **$5.00** Fresh and simple, nicely balanced between pear and floral fruit and a touch of herbs. **✪**

81 EHLERS GROVE Sauvignon Blanc Napa Valley 1994 **$9.50** Veers strongly toward the herbal side, offering a touch of green apple to balance the celery and herb flavors. Ready now.

81 FIRESTONE Sauvignon Blanc Santa Ynez Valley 1993 **$7.00** Strongly floral and distinctly herbal and peppery, showing enough bright fruit to balance things on the finish.

81 FORESTVILLE Sauvignon Blanc California 1994 **$5.50** Simple, fruity and refreshing, echoing apple and spice.

81 WILLIAM HILL Sauvignon Blanc Napa Valley Napa 1993 **$9.50** Smooth-textured, citrusy pear and floral flavors that linger.

81 JOULLIAN Sauvignon Blanc Carmel Valley 1994 **$9.00** Lots of mineral aromas and flavors come to the fore in this lean, spicy wine. A hint of oak on the finish.

81 CHARLES KRUG Sauvignon Blanc Napa Valley 1993 **$9.00** Crisp, floral, lightly fruity. Finishes smooth. Ready now.

81 LOUIS M. MARTINI Sauvignon Blanc Napa Valley 1994 **$8.00** Light and lean, adding a peachy edge to the modest floral flavors.

81 RAYMOND Sauvignon Blanc Napa Valley 1993 **$9.50** Spicy, floral flavors run through this straightforward, slightly vegetal wine.

80 BEAULIEU Sauvignon Blanc Napa Valley 1993 **$10.00** Bright and fruity, showing simple pear and mint flavors that finish a little short.

80 BRUTOCAO Sauvignon Blanc Mendocino 1994 **$9.50** Soft at first, citrusy-tart on the finish. A stewed onion edge doesn't compliment the pear flavors.

80 CANYON ROAD Sauvignon Blanc California 1995 **$7.00** Fresh and bright apple and pineapple flavors that narrow a bit on the finish.

80 DUNNEWOOD Sauvignon Blanc North Coast Barrel Select 1993 **$7.00** Light and simple, creamy enough to show off some nice pear and spice flavors.

80 GREENWOOD RIDGE Sauvignon Blanc Anderson Valley 1993 **$9.00** Earthy, minty flavors dominate this toasty wine, a little sharp with oak flavor on the finish ○

80 HONIG Sauvignon Blanc Napa Valley Barrel Fermented 1993 **$10.00** Herbal, vegetal notes tip this into the "odd" but good category.

80 OBESTER Sauvignon Blanc Mendocino County 1993 **$8.50** Slightly raisiny, earthy edge to the modest fruit keeps this a little off balance. Drinkable now.

80 RADANOVICH Sauvignon Blanc Sierra Foothills 1994 **$8.00** Simple, tart and minty, with a citrusy finish.

80 ST. SUPERY Sauvignon Blanc Napa Valley Dollarhide Ranch 1993 **$8.50** Simple and a little tired, but the grapefruit flavors persist on the finish. ○

80 TAFT STREET Sauvignon Blanc Sonoma County 1994 **$8.00** Soft, simple and generous, with interesting citrus accents.

OREGON

84 ASHLAND Sauvignon Blanc Rogue Valley 1993 **$7.50** Broad and almost plush, a generous wine with nicely modulated pear, caramel and floral flavors. Ready now.

80 AUTUMN WIND Sauvignon Blanc Oregon 1993 **$8.00** Soft and floral, plus a little peppery around the edges. Ready now.

Washington

87 CATERINA Sauvignon Blanc Columbia
Valley 1994 **$7.00** Bright and spicy, a lively wine
with nice sparks of citrus, green apple and peach, plus
an herbal zing on the finish.

87 BARNARD GRIFFIN Fumé Blanc Columbia
Valley 1994 **$9.00** Crisp and lively, sprightly with
juicy pear, citrus and delicate herb flavors that last on
the finish. Good fun and value.

87 LATAH CREEK Sauvignon Blanc Washington
1994 **$8.00** Smooth, lively and intriguing in the way it
weaves together its pear, apple, herb and vanilla flavors.

86 HOGUE Fumé Blanc Columbia Valley 1994
$7.50 Distinctly spicy and varietal, a touch of vanilla
echoing on the finish. This dry wine from Washington
offers a lot of character for its price. ✪

84 BALCOM & MOE Sauvignon Blanc
Washington 1994 **$9.00** Crisp and juicy, featuring
ripe pear, spice and a touch of green.

84 STATON HILLS Fumé Blanc Washington
1994 **$9.00** Light, crisp and fruity, with pear and
gentle spice flavors that persist nicely on the finish.

84 CHATEAU STE. MICHELLE Sauvignon
Blanc Columbia Valley 1993 **$9.00** Light, airy and
refreshing, adding a citrusy edge to the pear and faint-
ly herbal flavors. ✪

82 COLUMBIA Sauvignon Blanc Columbia
Valley 1994 **$8.00** Simple, austere, haylike notes.

82 FACELLI Fumé Blanc Columbia Valley 1993 **$9.00** Smooth and lightly floral; simple and graced by a touch of vanilla.

82 PAUL THOMAS Sauvignon Blanc Columbia Valley 1994 **$8.00** Very dry, austere, bordering on bitter, but refreshing in its crisp and citrusy intensity.

80 SILVER LAKE Fumé Blanc Columbia Valley Dry 1993 **$6.00** Smoky notes resembling toasted onion skins intrude on the spicy nectarine flavor, but the finish is fresh.

80 WASHINGTON HILLS Sauvignon Blanc Columbia Valley Varietal Select 1993 **$7.00** Doesn't quite come together, citrusy and sharp, but some raw nectarine flavor follows through as well.

Sauvignon Blend

California

87 BERINGER Sauvignon Blanc Sémillon Meritage Knights Valley 1993 **$9.00** A smooth and round Bordeaux-style white blend from this California winery. This is buttery, with just a touch of herb in the background under the honey and pear. Drinkable now.

86 LYETH Meritage White Sonoma County 1994 **$7.50** Crisp and fruity, with a floral thread runing through the green apple flavors. Ready now.

84 DE LORIMIER Spectrum Alexander Valley Meritage 1994 **$10.00** Definitely herbal, with a peppery edge to the modest fig and floral flavors.

82 DUCKHORN Migration White Napa Valley 1994 **$7.50** Austere, adding a lean edge to the onion and spice notes. Citric finish.

WASHINGTON

85 HEDGES Fumé-Chardonnay Columbia Valley 1994 **$6.50** Fruity and bright, light on its feet but zesty in its grapefruit and apple flavors.

Sémillon and Sémillon Blend

CALIFORNIA

86 CRESTON Chevrier Blanc Paso Robles 1994 **$9.00** Smooth and lavishly perfumed, a brightly appealing white that shows a nice touch of pear on the finish. This one calls itself by an alternate moniker for Sémillon, but has 20 percent Sauvignon in the mix.

83 ALDERBROOK Sémillon Dry Creek Valley 1993 **$8.50** Bright and fruity, a friendly wine with melon and tobacco flavors.

OREGON

81 SOKOL BLOSSER Semillon/Chardonnay Oregon NV **$9.00** Broad and flavorful, showing tobacco and smoky nuances to the ripe pear flavor.

Washington

88 COLUMBIA Sémillon Columbia Valley Chevrier Sur Lie 1994 **$9.00** Very pretty floral, citrusy flavors dance lightly on a delicate frame, then linger nicely on the finish.

86 CHATEAU STE. MICHELLE Sémillon Columbia Valley Barrel Fermented 1994 **$7.00** This Washington white is lively: The zingy flavors of spice, herb and pear show plenty of character and length. Delicious now and an unquestionable value.

85 COLUMBIA Sémillon Columbia Valley 1994 **$6.50** This is a lean and refreshing white, offering lively peach and floral flavors. A great value from Washington. Drinkable now.

85 COLUMBIA CREST Sémillon Columbia Valley 1994 **$6.00** Bright and citrusy, shaded by a touch of smoke and tobacco, finishing buttery and smooth. A bargain from Washington made to enjoy now. ✪

85 HOGUE Sémillon Columbia Valley 1994 **$7.50** Round-textured, generous in flavor, spicy and toasty, adding a citrusy edge on the finish. Ready now.

84 ARBOR CREST Sémillon Columbia Valley Dionysus Vineyard 1994 **$6.50** Light, Crisp and a little floral, turning toward apple and spice on the finish.

84 COLUMBIA Sémillon-Chardonnay Washington 1994 **$8.00** Toasty, spicy flavors dominate this smooth and engaging white. Drinkable now.

84 COLUMBIA CREST Sémillon-Chardonnay Columbia Valley 1994 **$7.00** Lean, floral and fragrant, balanced by just enough citrusy fruit.

82 CHATEAU STE. MICHELLE Sémillon Columbia Valley 1993 **$7.00** Soft and harmonious, showing some nice pear and tobacco notes.

81 SNOQUALMIE Sémillon Columbia Valley 1994 **$6.00** Crisp, light and distinctly herbal, finishing delicately and with a touch of pear.

Seyval Blanc

WASHINGTON

86 HOGUE Seyval Blanc Columbia Valley 1994 **$7.50** Ripe and tasty, striking a balance between apple and pear flavors and nice hints of herb and spice. Ready now.

85 BADGER MOUNTAIN Seyval Blanc Columbia Valley Sevé Certified Organic Vineyard 1994 **$6.00** Bright and flavorful, floral and lively, echoing pear and a bit of vanilla on the long finish.

84 COLUMBIA Seyval Blanc Washington 1994 **$8.00** Toasty, spicy flavors dominate this smooth, engaging wine, ready now.

83 PAUL THOMAS Seyval Blanc Washington 1994 **$8.00** Firm and flavorful, stuffed with melon and herb notes that take a turn toward austere on the finish.

82 WASHINGTON HILLS Seyval Blanc Columbia Valley Varietal Select 1993 **$7.00** Strange medicinal flavors run through this pineapple-scented white, lingering juicily on the finish. Ready now.

OTHER U.S.

87 NAVARRO Pinot Gris Anderson Valley 1993 **$8.50** Smooth, polished and creamy, lovely for its peach and orange cream flavors that linger delicately on the finish.

82 UNIONVILLE VINEYARDS Seyval Blanc New Jersey Windfall 1994 **$9.00** Aggressive toasty, smoky oak flavors overwhelm the fruit in this thick, chewy wine. Though a bit startling at first sip, it grows on you, finishing with pretty pineapple notes. Unbalanced but appealing.

80 BOORDY Seyval Blanc Maryland Sur Lie Reserve 1993 **$8.00** Smooth and thick, this offers apple cider and light piney notes, with some vanilla oak accents. It's balanced but a bit dull.

Other White Varietals

85 MARTIN BROTHERS Muscat Paso Robles Allegro Moscato 1994 **$10.00** Lightly sparkling, sweet and fruity, featuring a definite peppery-floral flavor that lingers on the finish. Drink soon.

84 ZILLAH OAKES Aligoté Yakima Valley 1993 **$10.00** Crisp, refreshing, lively apple and citrus flavors, finishing simple and clean as a whistle. Ready now.

83 AIRLIE Müller Thurgau Oregon 1995 **$6.50** Light and frankly sweet, with delicate peach and apple flavors and a gentle finish.

83 PAUL THOMAS Lemberger Columbia Valley 1993 **$8.00** Light and fruity, offering simple, charming, spicy berry flavors and a touch of walnut.

82 IVAN TAMAS Pinot Grigio Monterey 1993 **$9.00** Simple, broad and a little spicy, picking up an almond edge to the modest peach flavors. Drinkable now.

81 ARCIERO Muscat Paso Robles 1994 **$6.50** Light, soft and decidely floral, sporting a peppery edge to the modest pear flavor.

Other Whites

86 CA' DEL SOLO Big House White California 1994 **$7.50** Light and fragrant like a Muscat, but with extra citrus and somewhat underripe peach notes to make it more interesting. Finishes dry. A good price for a pleasant white.

85 CA' DEL SOLO Malvasia Bianca Monterey 1994 **$8.50** Soft and broad, a mouthful of fresh pear and spicy grape flavors. Drink soon, though.

83 ELLISTON Cuvée des Trois Sunol Valley Vineyard Central Coast 1993 **$10.00** Sturdy, spicy, straightforward white, round and slightly honeyed, more distinctive for its structure and texture than for its flavors. Ready now.

83 WORDEN Oyster White Washington 1992 **$9.00** Light and simple, a little spicy, a little toasty, finishing with an almond and peach character. Drink now.

82 CHADDSFORD Spring Wine Pennsylvania 1994 **$8.50** A rich, off-dry white with apple and honey flavors and good acidity. Clean and refreshing.

81 HIDDEN CELLARS Chauché Gris Organically Grown Grapes Mendocino 1994 **$8.00** Soft, vaguely spicy in flavor, a simple white with enough roundness to carry the modest fruit and cream notes.

BLUSH

CALIFORNIA

83 MCDOWELL Grenache Rosé Mendocino 1993 **$7.00** There's plenty of dried fruit and spice in the aromas and flavors, underscored by lively acidity. Vibrant and refreshing; a substantial finish.

83 RUTHERFORD ESTATE White Zinfandel California 1994 **$7.00** Off-dry, showing nice cherry and berry notes. Has some body and balance and loads of good fruit aromas and flavors. Clean, well made; good dose of apricot on the finish.

82 BONNY DOON Blush California Vin Gris de Cigare Pink Wine 1994 **$7.50** Rosé-style, but adding a little spritz. Very dry and almost austere, offering dried currant and herbal flavors. Well balanced.

82 HEITZ Grignolino Napa Valley Rosé 1994 **$5.50** A serious wine that tastes like a rosé. Its wild side is dominated by earthy, spicy berry flavors. Extremely pungent and dry as well as full-bodied.

82 MIRASSOU White Zinfandel California 1994 **$10.00** Very fruity, offering some body and zippy acidity. Only a hint of sweetness; nice strawberry and cherry flavors.

81 BERINGER White Zinfandel California 1994 **$5.50** Flavorful, sweet and fruity, featuring decent cherry and berry notes. There's enough acidity here to make it balanced.

81 VENDANGE White Zinfandel California Autumn Harvest 1994 **$6.00** A wine showing some character. Smells and tastes like Muscat with an herbal note. Flavors linger on the finish.

80 FETZER White Zinfandel California 1994 **$7.00** Sweeter style yielding strawberry flavors and a hint of butter on the finish. It has enough acidity to balance the sugar.

80 DOMAINE DE LA TERRE ROUGE Blush Fiddletown Vin Gris d'Amador 1994 **$9.00** Light, simple and crisp; not sweet but not particularly flavorful either.

80 M.G. VALLEJO White Zinfandel California 1994 **$6.00** Well made, tasting of tea and cherry. Quite dry and in balance, but fairly soft.

Other U.S.

85 KIONA Vintage Rosé Washington 1993 **$6.00** Fruity, generous and popping in cherry and vaguely cinnamonlike flavors, finishing on the dry side. Don't drink this too cold.

83 BILTMORE ESTATE White Zinfandel North Carolina American Zinfandel Blanc de Noir 1994 **$6.00** Dried cherry and watermelon flavors dominate this well-made wine. It has some body with good acidity. Overall, a refreshing and tasty quaff.

82 PRESTON WINE CELLARS Blush Washington Gamay Beaujolais Rosé 1994 **$5.00** Light and effusively fruity, sporting lively raspberry and watermelon flavors and finishing slightly sweet.

82 YAKIMA RIVER Lemberger Sof/Lem Yakima Valley 1995 **$8.50** A simple and dryish rosé. Appealing raspberry and rhubarb flavors linger on the finish.

Sparkling

Oregon

85 SILVER LAKE Brut Willamette Valley NV **$10.00** Delicate in texture, subtly flavored, echoing pear, toast and floral notes on the finish.

WASHINGTON

87 DOMAINE STE. MICHELLE Blanc de Blanc Columbia Valley NV **$10.00** Toasty, spicy flavors characterize this crisp sparkler from Washington. An appealing price, and it's made for drinking now. ✺

DESSERT

CALIFORNIA

84 GEYSER PEAK Johannisberg Riesling California Soft 1995 **$7.00** Fresh and openly sweet, this is nicely balanced to show off the peach, spice and floral flavors on a polished frame. Good, typical flavors for this grape at a bargain.

84 SUTTER HOME Muscat Alexandria California 1994 **$5.00** Light and sweet, but a generous wine for this price. Pours out its spicy pear and litchi flavors on the palate. Drink it as, or with, dessert. ✺

83 GAINEY Johannisberg Riesling Santa Barbara County 1995 **$9.00** Soft, sweet and generous with its citrusy peach and lightly floral aromas and flavors.

82 EBERLE Muscat Canelli Paso Robles 1994 **$9.00** Light, sweet and simple, a solid wine of delicate litchi flavors that needs light dessert fare to balance it.

81 GAN EDEN Gewürztraminer Late Harvest Monterey County 1993 **$8.50** Frankly sweet, offering peach and apricot flavors that fade a little on the finish.

80 BRINDIAMO Muscat Alexandria San Diego County Moscato Aromatico Limited Bottling 1994 **$6.00** Despite perfumey, almost soapy aromas, it's a simple, lightly sweet, drinkable dessert wine.

OREGON

87 FORIS Pinot Noir Oregon Ruby 1993 **$10.00** Has Port-like color and aromas, but seems lighter in the mouth. A gentle wine with appealing berry, currant and spice flavors that linger nicely. Best from 1998.

86 KNUDSEN ERATH White Riesling Late Harvest Willamette Valley 1994 **$8.00** Bright, fruity and freshly sweet, like biting into a fresh peach, complete with the fuzzy texture on the finish.

WASHINGTON

93 CHATEAU STE. MICHELLE White Riesling Late Harvest Columbia Valley Chateau Reserve 1991 **$9.00** A ripe, sweet, generous and elegant dessert wine from Washington. The silky mouth-feel and gorgeous honey, apricot and spice flavors blend beautifully, joined by a touch of almond on the lovely finish. Wonderful now, and it should last through 1999 and beyond.

91 COVEY RUN White Riesling Late Harvest Yakima Valley 1994 **$7.00** This is sweet and brilliantly focused, wrapping its intense apricot, pear and honey flavors in a sheen of sweet spices. Such distinctiveness makes this an almost inconceivable deal. Delicious now.

88 HOGUE White Riesling Late Harvest Columbia Valley 1994 **$6.00** This Riesling is frankly sweet, but crisply balanced. It keeps the ripe apricot, honey and citrus flavors humming. Offers style and complexity for an agreeable price. Drinkable now.

88 STEWART Gewüztraminer Late Harvest Yakima Valley 1994 **$8.50** Sweet and beguiling bite-of-fresh-peach immediacy, finishing with a touch of apricot and distinctive spice. Delicious now.

87 TAGARIS Johannisberg Riesling Columbia Valley Reserve 1994 **$6.00** Ripe, generous sweet apricot and pear flavors, delicately balanced to show off the fruit without presenting too much sweetness. Ready now.

85 ARBOR CREST Muscat Canelli Columbia Valley 1994 **$6.50** A frankly sweet dessert wine with rich pear, litchi and gentle spice flavors. Drink while it's still fresh.

85 HYATT Black Muscat Yakima Valley 1994 **$7.00** More spicy flavor than aroma in this lightly sweet pink wine that gives up more generous cinnamon and strawberry flavors on the long finish.

85 KIONA White Riesling Late Harvest Yakima Valley 1994 **$6.50** Sweet and fresh-tasting, showing peach and hints of apricot. On the light side for such a sweet wine.

85 SEVEN HILLS White Riesling Columbia Valley 1994 **$7.00** Simple and easy to drink, like biting into a juicy peach; adds resiny overtones on the finish. Ready now.

85 PAUL THOMAS Johannisberg Riesling Columbia Valley Select Harvest 1994 **$6.00** Frankly sweet, but still light enough to show off its lightly honeyed pear and pretty floral flavors.

84 ZILLAH OAKES Riesling Late Harvest Yakima Valley 1993 **$9.00** Definitely sweet but light in texture, sporting honey, earth, tobacco and pear flavors that are more like Sémillon than Riesling.

83 TUCKER Muscat Canelli Yakima Valley 1993 **$7.00** Soft and gently fruity, showing a modest level of distinctive Muscat flavor lingering on the finish.

82 SNOQUALMIE Muscat Canelli Columbia Valley 1994 **$8.00** Simple, sweet but not quite syrupy. Generous pear and litchi flavors follow through on the lingering finish.

81 COVEY RUN Muscat Yakima Valley Morio Muskat 1994 **$7.00** Not too sweet, a dessert wine showing delicate spice and floral overtones to the modest fruit.

81 WASHINGTON HILLS White Riesling Columbia Valley Varietal Select Special Harvest 1993 **$7.00** Tries to be crisply balanced, but lacks the intensity to show much fruit up front. Has some nice spicy notes on the finish.

80 LATAH CREEK Muscat Canelli Washington 1994 **$6.00** Sweet and simple, soft-textured, offering subtle grapey, spicy flavors.

Other Countries

Outside the traditional appellations of Europe and the more established New World regions such as California and even Chile, there are many more places in the world where wine bargains can be found.

One of the best is Argentina. While close to Chile's major wine producing regions, Argentina's vineyards are just now emerging amid a more open and stable political system. Meanwhile, look for wines with the Mendoza appellation, including the Trapiche Malbec Oak Cask Vintner's Selection and Etchart's Malbec.

Central and eastern Europe also have some values. Look for the Boutari Red Naoussa from Greece, and from Bulgaria try Bulgare's Merlot and Pinot Noir blend at the astonishing price of $4.

Argentina

R ed

87 TRAPICHE Malbec Mendoza Oak Cask
Vintner's Selection Lujan de Coyo County 1991
$8.00 Oodles of ripe black currant flavors are marked
by sweet American oak, lending immense appeal. This
Argentine version of the French variety is straightforward, with good balance and structure. A good value
and drinkable now. ✪

84 ETCHART Malbec Mendoza 1993 **$6.00**
There's plenty of blackberry and black cherry fruit
here, and lean tannins add backbone. It's straightforward and clean.

83 PASCUAL TOSO Malbec Mendoza 1994
$6.00 Ripe and jammy, this shows blackberry and
plum flavors with hints of game and smoke. Lush and
drinkable, but without much tannin, it goes down easy.

82 PASCUAL TOSO Cabernet Sauvignon
Mendoza 1992 **$8.00** Showing some age now, this
layers tea and smoke flavors on top of the cherry core.
It's silky, but still has tannin; best with light foods.

81 VALENTIN BIANCHI Malbec Mendoza Elsa's
Vineyard 1992 **$5.00** Lively black pepper notes
perk up the black cherry flavor. Tannins are somewhat
strong for the fruit, but it can handle simple meat
dishes. Drinkable now. ✪

✪ = Widest availability (over 15,000 cases produced)

Bulgaria

RED

84 BULGARE Merlot & Pinot Noir Sliven 1993
$4.00 An unbelievably great value from Bulgaria.
Generous in flavor, easygoing in texture, with light
tannins and good fruit flavors. This has fresh cherry
and raspberry accents and an enticing balance. ✪

84 HASKOVO ESTATES Merlot Haskovo 1993
$5.50 A resinous quality runs through this Bulgarian
wine that has decent plum and black currant flavors.
Good and fruity-offering a lot in this price range-with
a mouth-filling texture and a spicy finish.

83 CHATEAU DALINA Merlot Russe 1994 **$5.00**
Satisfying but not complex. There's a good focus to
the nice cherry, plum and berry flavors. Also a good
touch of spice, with a tart, zingy finish.

82 CHATEAU DALINA Cabernet Sauvignon
Russe 1994 **$5.00** Fruity and fresh, with raspberry
and sweet cherry flavors and a hint of tobacco. Light
and drinkable now.

Greece

RED

84 BOUTARI Red Naoussa 1993 **$8.00** Crisp,
solidly made, somewhat tannic, showing enough
depth in the berry and anise flavors to keep it interesting. Nicely balanced to drink now.

82 BOUTARI Red Nemea 1993 **$8.00** A ripe-tasting red that's fairly lush and fruity, offering spicy accents and medium body. Soft and not too tannic; drink now while it's fresh. ✪

81 CAVA TSANTALIS Red Greece 1990 **$7.00** Sturdy, showing a lean, moderately tannic texture and modest fruit character.

Index of
Winery Names